Operation EBENSBURG:
SOE's Austrian 'Bonzos' and the rescue of looted European art

Bernard O'Connor

Bernard O'Connor

Copyright © 2018 Bernard O'Connor
All rights reserved.

Attempts have been made to locate, contact and acknowledge copyright holders of quotes and illustrations used in my work. They have all been credited within the text and in the bibliography. Much appreciation is given to those who have agreed that I include their work. Any copyright owners who are not properly identified and acknowledged, get in touch so that I may make any necessary corrections.
Small parts of this book may be reproduced in similar academic works providing due acknowledgement is given in the introduction and within the text. Any errors or suggested additions can be forwarded to me for future editions.

ISBN: 978-0-244-38089-2

Operation EBENSBURG was 'one of the most significant missions undertaken by SOE, one that would ultimately prove to be of the utmost importance in saving some of Europe's most precious art treasures from destruction... one of the most heroic single episodes in the entire war.' (Harclerode, Peter and Pittaway, Brendan, *The Lost Masters: WW II and the Looting of Europe's Treasurehouses*, Welcome Rain Publishers, 2000, p.99)

List of Contents

Foreword
Introduction
Albrecht Gaiswinkler, the leader of Operation EBENSBURG
Protecting Europe's works of art during the war
Gaiswinkler's continued training: October 1944 to February 1945
Alfred Sommer, Operation EBENSBURG's wireless operator
The other members of the EBENSBURG team
Karl Standhartinger's training: October 1944 to February 1945
Karl Lzicar's training: October 1944 to February 1945
Joseph Grafl, EBENSBURG's replacement wireless operator
The EBENSBURG team in 'Maryland' February to April 1944
The flight to Austria: 8 April 1945
The EBENSBURG team's arrival and their first weeks in Austria
The arrival of the Americans and the rescue of the stolen artworks
Gaiswinkler's help in the Americans' arrest of leading Nazi officials
The EBENSBURG team after the German surrender in May 1945

Bernard O'Connor

Foreword

While researching Allied sabotage operations in Western Europe during the Second World War, I learnt that the Axis forces had their own sabotage schools and trained saboteurs to attack Allied targets, not just in Europe. When some of these German-trained saboteurs were captured, they were brought to England for interrogation, not just for their intelligence, but also in the hope that they could be 'turned' and work for the Allies.

I was able to locate and read copies of these men and women's interrogation reports kept in the National Archives in Kew, and learned that the Allies had obtained valuable intelligence about their schools, their instructors, their syllabus, their methods, the sabotage equipment they used, their targets and how they were infiltrated and exfiltrated. I also learned that the Germans had captured many Allied saboteurs and the Abwehr, their military intelligence service, acquired similar intelligence through interrogation, often involving bribery or torture.

When I was looking through a folder of documents generated by the Field Security Section operating in Italy to find evidence of German-trained Italian saboteurs, I found a memorandum from the Counter Intelligence Section of the 11 US Armoured Division sent to their British counterparts in Italy. On entering Western Austria in June 1945, they had met Albrecht Gaiswinkler who claimed to have been born in 1905 in Bad Aussee, a spa town near Graz, and to have been employed as an explosives expert by the British Secret Service with the aliases Alfred Winkler and George Schumacher. It added that he had been flown to Italy on 4 April 1945 and parachuted behind enemy lines near Bad Aussee on 8 April with three other men and a radio transmitter. (TNA WO204/11987, 16 June 1945)

Having read nothing on sabotage operations in Austria during my years of research, I was intrigued. If Gaiswinkler had been engaged by the British Secret Service, I knew it was likely to have been a Special Operations Executive (SOE) mission. Set up in 1940, the SOE was a top-secret intelligence service which recruited, trained, equipped and infiltrated organisers, wireless operators, couriers, weapons instructors, saboteurs and assassins behind enemy lines. They also arranged their exfiltration, researched and developed wireless telegraphy, weapons, explosives and sabotage equipment and engaged in the production and dissemination of propaganda material. Their officers liaised with other British intelligence services like MI5 and MI6, other Allied governments-in-exile and their intelligence services, the War Office, the Ministry of Economic Warfare, the British Army, the Royal Air Force, the Royal Navy and the BBC. They had Country Sections and their own Security Service.

As many of their agents' personnel files and mission reports have been declassified since the 2000 Freedom of Information Act, I entered Gaiwsinker's name into the Discovery search engine on the National Archives website and was surprised when his file reference appeared. I need to thank their staff for their efforts in making historians' searches so much easier than searching catalogues.

Thanks to Steven Kippax of the Yahoo SOE forum, within an hour of enquiring, I was able to read Gaiswinkler's file. It revealed that he had been working in the Luftwaffe's administrative section in France, defected to the French resistance and handed himself into American troops in France after the Normandy landings. Interrogated by American counter-intelligence staff, from what he told them, they decided to send him to England with the recommendation that he would be a suitable agent to be trained by the SOE and infiltrated into Austria. There was no indication of what he told them that justified their recommendation.

Research by ex-journalist and TV producer Charles de Jaeger, ex-soldier and author Peter Harclerode, investigative journalist Brendan Pittaway and art historian and author Noah Charney revealed that he had intelligence related to the Nazis hiding an estimated $500,000 worth of stolen artworks in the Altaussee salt mines. These mines were close to his hometown of Bad Aussee, northwest Austria. While these authors' focus was on the artworks, they were able to access Gaiswinkler's post-war memoirs and interviewed him, the pilot and one of the crew of the plane that flew him and three others into Austria in April 1945, his wireless operator and others in the Bad Aussee area. They shed light on what SOE called Operation EBENSBURG. Wikipedia's English and German webpages and the Special Forces Roll of Honour provided additional, sometimes contradictory details. I need to acknowledge the assistance of Professor Peter Pirker who has researched SOE agents in Austria. The following websites provided additional details and illustrations: CIA, forgottenairfields, lootedartwork, furtherglory, Youtube, Wikipedia, ooegeschichte, static2 and army.cz.

Introduction

All foreigners entering Britain during the war were interrogated to ascertain whether they were enemy agents and to obtain political, military, economic and other intelligence of interest to the Allied war effort. Male civilians were sent to the Royal Victoria Patriotic School in Wandsworth, London, and females to Nightingale House, Clapham, London, known collectively as the 'London Reception Centre'.

Following the Allied Invasion of France in June 1944, many captured enemy personnel were flown to RAF Northolt near London and interned in Kempston Park prisoner of war camps. Those who convinced their interrogators that they were anti-Nazi and were 'turned', willing to work with the Allies as double agents, were sent to Tyting House, St Martha, near Guildford, where they would have been provided with clothes, P.T. kit, plimsolls, battledress and boots. They were then taken to Bellasis House, a requisitioned mansion with extensive grounds on Box Hill Road, near Dorking, Surrey. For those in the Intelligence Service, it was known as Special Training School (STS) 2 while for others it was known as 'Camp 99A'.' Germans, Russians, Poles and Austrians underwent paramilitary training with German-speaking officers from SOE's X Section, which was responsible for Germany and Austria. They wanted to identify those who showed potential to be employed as organisers, wireless operators and saboteurs and parachuted back into enemy-occupied territory (EOT).

Codenamed 'Bonzos', X Section was involved with the administration and planning of their missions. SOE's Training Section provided them with the same paramilitary and clandestine warfare training they gave their other agents but to avoid other nationalities discovering that the British were sending captured enemy troops back into occupied Europe, they had to be trained in separate establishments.

Modern-day photographs of front and back view of Bellasis Manor (STS 2), Box Hill Road, near Guildford, Surrey, where 'Bonzos' were given paramilitary warfare training. (www.travelblog.org.org/Photos/5878068; Courtesy of Paul McCue)

Operation EBENSBURG

Contemporary photograph of Czech First Lieutenant Hrubrec with Sten gun Mk II outside "Bellasis Villa", near Dorking, Surrey, where SOE's 'Bonzos' were trained 1944-1945. (http://www.army.cz/images/id_7001_8000/7419/assassination-

Wanborough Manor (STS 5), near Guildford, Surrey, where 'Bonzos' were given paramilitary training 1944-1945. (Courtesy of Paul McCue)

Bernard O'Connor

Undated photographs of Albrecht Gaiswinkler, Austrian 'saboteur' and resistance fighter. (Top: http://blogs.artinfo.com/outtakes/2015/03/24/fifa-art-stashed-in-castles-and-salt-mines/ Bottom: http://www.specialforcesroh.com/gallery.php)

Operation EBENSBURG

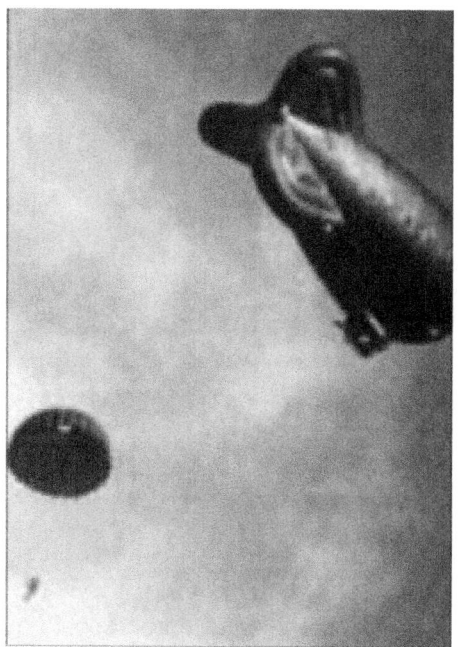

A parachutist dropping from an air balloon, http://www.army.cz/images/id_7001_8000/7419/assassination-en.pdf

A parachutist dropping from a Whitley bomber. (http://www.army.cz/images/id_7001_8000/7419/assassination-en.pdf)

Bernard O'Connor

Gumley Hall (STS 44), near Market Harborough, Leicestershire, where 'Bonzo's' were provided with clandestine warfare training. (http://leicestershirelalala.com/ralph-hollingworth-our-top-brass-in-soe/)

Josef Grafl, the EBENSBURG team's wireless operator (Clip from 'Hitlers Schatz im Berg')

Operation EBENSBURG

https://www.vacationstogo.com/cruise_port/Bari__Italy.cfm

Bernard O'Connor

Albrecht Gaiswinkler, the leader of Operation EBENSBURG

On 24 September 1944, Gaiswinkler was 'Put through the Cards', the term used by the Security Section for vetting by MI5, Britain's domestic security agency, and 'C', the code name for MI6, the overseas security agency. A search of their intelligence files on enemy personnel and 'Most Secret Sources', intercepted enemy wireless communications done at Britain's Code and Cypher School at Bletchley Park, Buckinghamshire, revealed 'No Trace'. Finding nothing that suggested he was an enemy agent, a note in his file from the Operating Commander Richardson of 'Group C' at Bellasis stated that 'Gaiswinkler has now been selected to undergo training at STS 5.' To avoid anyone being able to identify his real name, he had to use the alias, Alfred Winkler. (TNA HS9/553/3, 2 October 1944)

STS 5 was Wanborough Manor, another isolated country house near Guildford in Surrey, which had been requisitioned and used from January 1941 to assess students' suitability for further SOE training. From July 1944, the manor was used to provide paramilitary training for the 'Bonzos'. Not wanting German-speaking students to be seen or heard at Brickendonbury Manor where the SOE taught specialist industrial sabotage, the Bonzos were provided with demolition training in the theory and practice of explosives, detonators, time delays etc. at Wanborough. There were also physical training exercises and lessons in Morse, map reading, orienteering, fieldcraft (outdoor survival), camouflage, weapons practice with Sten guns, pistols and grenades, even jumping off moving trains.

Little has come to light about conditions in what was called the 'Periwig School' except that students wore British battledress, were free to walk in the grounds but not allowed to leave unless escorted by a conducting officer. The men slept in dormitories on camp beds. All food was provided in the canteen. They were given beer and cigarette rations of 3 shillings (£0.15) a day. Trips were arranged to the local swimming baths and cinema, but no English money was allowed, suggesting their admission tickets were bought for them. Medical check-ups were provided, and visits to the hospital or a dentist were arranged when necessary. To identify important machinery to be

Operation EBENSBURG

sabotaged, escorted visits were made to the Guildford Telephone Exchange and local locomotive sheds. Lights out were at 23.00 hours. (TNA HS8/883)

Gaiswinkler's records show that he was No. 9 of 18 Bonzo students from Group 12 who were sent to Wanborough. Sergeant Hartog, the German-speaking conducting officer in the Field Security Police who 'escorted' Gaiswinkler and acted as his translator, was expected to write regular character and progress reports. His first report, dated 10 October, identified him as a 38-year-old, 'typical Austrian type', 5ft 11½" tall and weighing 187 pounds; brown hair, thin on top; brown eyes; long face and well-built with an appendicitis scar.

He was born on 29 October 1905 in Bad Aussee, a small spa town in Salzkammergut in the Totes Gebirge mountain range of western Styria, a province in Southeast Austria, about 80km east of Salzburg and the German frontier. He grew up at Eselsbach 76, Bad Aussee, with his father, Franz, a retired salt-mine worker, mother, Anna, and three brothers, a postal official, an electrician, and one who was still at home. Unlike him, they had all been excused military service. After leaving Burgerschule, he had worked in the timber business, on the railways and farms before becoming a civil servant, an 'ober inspector' in social insurance at der Krankenkasse, Graz, the Styrian capital. He was married with two children and lived in Graz where he enjoyed athletics, sailing, making radios and reading. (TNA HS9/553/3)

Whether he told Hartog about his political beliefs was not mentioned, but research by art historian professor Noah Charney who had access to Gaiswinkler's memoirs stated that his father had been a salt miner and that during the 1930s Gaiswinkler had been an active union supporter and a member of the Social Democratic Party. 'Most importantly, he was a steadfast anti-Nazi, serving some months in prison in 1934 for his political dissension. He joined the regional underground Resistance in 1938, and eventually, his activities drew the attention of the Gestapo. To avoid imprisonment, Gaiswinkler enlisted in the Luftwaffe on 20 March 1943.' (Charney, Noah, *Stealing the Mystic Lamb: The True Story of the World's Most Coveted Masterpiece*, Public Affairs, New York, 2012)

According to Hartog, he served in Holland, Belgium and France, but gave no details. His personnel file reported him serving three months with the Luftwaffe's 'Flieger Ausbuildings

Regiment 90, Battalion. HQ. (Q side)'. Following a failed application for an officer's course as Paymaster at St Brieux, he claimed that he had been given office work for a year, somewhere on the outskirts of Paris.

He told me how with the help of the Mayor of St Jouen [Saint Jouan-des-Guerets, about 10km south of St Malo] when staying with 4 wagons of ammunition at this place, he deliberately prepared engine trouble and remained there 1 week. He arranged with the Mayor and the aid of local French men that the 14 Nazis who were with him on this convoy were chased off and he handed the entire load over to the French Maquis. He remained 6 weeks with the French Resistance Movement [from 1 August] and on 15 September 44 went over to the Americans at Dinan [about 20km south of St Malo]. He speaks German with an Austrian accent and does not speak English. He is a little slow in his movements, but takes interest during lectures. He is very fond of sports and very keen on reading books. He is a willing worker.' (HS9/553/3, 10 October 1944)

He provided more details about his defection in his memoirs which were reported by Charney, Harclerode and Pittaway. Witnessing the execution of members of the French resistance prompted him to desert in the spring of 1944 when his unit moved to Paris and he subsequently reported making contact with the Maquis, one of France's underground guerrilla resistance movements. At the request of the German authorities, in March 1943, Pierre Laval, the Prime Minister of Vichy France, introduced the Service du Travail Obligitaire, compulsory work service. As many German men were engaged in military duties, all French men had to register their births. Those between nineteen and thirty-two were sent to work on the Atlantic Wall, in factories in Germany or on the Russian front. As the Germans expected 500,000 in the first six months, every week, about 20,000 were picked up on the streets of Paris. To avoid having to work for the Germans, many thousands of young men gave up work, left home and went to live in the woods and forests in the remote hills and mountains and formed resistance groups. Known as the Maquis after the Mediterranean vegetation amongst which many groups hid in the South of France, the SOE dropped organisers, couriers, wireless operators, weapons instructors, saboteurs, sabotage instructors and assassins as well as arms, ammunition, explosives and other supplies. Under Allied command, the SOE agents worked with these groups and coordinated action against the occupying German forces. SOE's X Section planned similar missions for Austrian 'Bonzos' to work with the Austrian Resistance

To avoid his family suffering recriminations, Gaiswinkler managed to vanish from his unit by trading identity papers and identity tag with a bomb victim who had been disfigured beyond recognition. He joined the Maquis with a stolen haul that included half a million francs and four trucks of arms and ammunition. In September of that year he and sixteen other German prisoners surrendered themselves to American soldiers of the U.S. Third Army at Dinan.

In his first post-capture interrogation, he must have convincingly expressed his strong anti-Nazi inclinations. More importantly, he told de Jaeger in the early 1960s that he had learnt from the letters sent to him from home that 'weekly convoys of trucks stacked with wooden crates were seen driving through the village at night in the direction of the salt mines. The area had been placed out of bounds to the villagers and was guarded by heavily armed men.' His father had worked in the Alt Aussee salt-mines, about 5km north of his hometown, which had been used since Roman times. He also reported being told that local inhabitants had heard loud explosions coming from the direction of Töplitzee, a large lake about 12km east of Bad Aussee. (de Jaeger, Charles. The Linz File: Hitler's Plunder of Europe's Art. London: Webb & Bower, 1981, p.125)

Protecting Europe's works of art during the war

Like the British stored the nation's valuable artwork in Welsh slate mines during the Second World War, the Austrians protected their artistic heritage underground. Hofrat Professor Herman Michel, whose opposition to Geobbel's plans to install an exhibition of Aryan superiority and derogation of inferior races had led to him being demoted from Head of Vienna's Natural History Museum to head the Mineralogy Department, in 1942 was in charge of the Viennese Service for the Protection of Historical Monuments.

Having visited the Altaussee salt mine to establish whether the disused sections would be suitable for storage, he recommended its use. Salt mining had been in operation in the Altaussee area for over 3,000 years, extracted by pumping water into the rock to dissolve the salt and evaporating the extracted brine. An extensive system of tunnels and caverns were an ideal hiding place.

It was noticed during the inspection that, in a small chapel hewn out of the salt rock wall of a cave the wooden altarpiece and decorations of green fir were in perfect condition though they had been neglected for years. The steady temperature [between 40 - 47°F (4.4° - 8.3°C)] and right degree of humidity [about 65%] made the mine an ideal storage place. Subsequently, electric lighting was installed, and wooden tiers were erected to hold the paintings. As soon as the storehouse was ready, the most valuable works of art from the Vienna museums were packed into it, safe from the Allied bombing.' (Ibid; Charney, op.cit. p.248)

Following the outbreak of war, Sir Leonard Woolley, the renowned archaeologist and curator of the Ashmolean Museum at Oxford, corresponded with archaeological and art institutions on the continent to compile lists of monuments and artworks that were under threat from the Nazis. The intelligence he gathered established that works of art, including those belonging to German citizens, were being confiscated by the Nazis in the occupied countries. Through barter and sale overseas, this stolen art became one of the Reich's major sources of income. (Charney, op.cit. p.211)

The Americans were also concerned about the loss of artwork. Fearing a Japanese invasion, in March 1941 a Committee of Conservation of Cultural Resources was set up. Two years later, Spring 1943, curators in American museums and art galleries started a programme to train officers to protect art and monuments in conflict zones. Known as the Monuments Fine Arts and Archives (MFAA),' or the 'Monuments Men', its staff included a few women but were mostly middle-aged men whose careers as art historians, architects, museum curators and professors were interrupted to help the Allied war effort. They were sent into occupied Europe with the American forces after the Allied invasion of France in an endeavour to protect all cultural heritage in the wake of warfare. A month after Italy's surrender in September 1943 and the German retreat northwards, the British War Office appointed Woolley as their archaeological adviser in the recovery and protection of artworks found in the expected liberated countries. He would have been in contact with Professor Paul Vaucher, the cultural attaché at the French embassy in London, who, in April 1944, headed the Commission for the Protection and Restitution of Cultural Material which documented cases of stolen artworks. The following month, Winston Churchill ordered the establishment of the 'British Committee of the Preservation and Restitution of Works of Art, Archives, and Other Material in Enemy Hands' under Lord Hugh Pattison-Macmillan's supervision and Woolley was appointed as its civilian leader.

Some Germans had concerns about their own artworks in times of war. In Peter Harclerode and Brendan Pittaway's *Lost Masters*, they mention that following the wanton destruction of Polish artworks by German troops, in 1940 the Nazi government established the Kuntschutz organisation to prevent similar destruction and looting in other occupied countries. Although its stated aim was to protect the enemy's art and return it after the war, Hitler secretly set up the Einsatzstab-Reichsleiter Rosenberg (ERR) to select items to be housed in the proposed Führermuseum in Linz, Austria. The Kuntschutz's representative in Paris, Dr Herman Bunjes, as well as helping catalogue items, oversaw the 'exchange' and 'loan' of artworks for Nazi Party leader Hermann Göring's private collection. (Harclerode, Peter & Pittaway, Brendan, *The Lost Masters: The Looting of Europe's Treasurehouses*, Orion, 2000, pp.26, 58-60, 92, 101;

In December 1944, Woolley, appointed Lieutenant Colonel, recommended to Lord Macmillan that His Britannic Majesty's Government take anticipatory action to protect artworks in occupied Europe. He had learned from Dr Max Göring, an art historian and member of the Bavarian Commission for the Preservation of Art and Monuments, that Hitler had ordered the destruction of all historic buildings and works of art in Germany to stop them falling into Allied hands. Several deposits in France had already been burned, and the German Commander of the Hague had told city officials that when the Allies arrived there would only be ruins. (TNA T209/10, 2

December 1944)
Fearing the advancing Russian, American and British armies would capture the looted artwork, on 19 March 1945, Hitler issued his 'Destructive Measures on Reich Territory'. Nicknamed the 'Nero Decree', it was an order for the complete destruction of Germany's infrastructure.

The struggle for the very existence of our people forces us to seize any means which can weaken the combat preparedness of our opponents and prevent them from advancing. Every opportunity, whether direct or indirect, to inflict the most resonant possible damage on the enemy's ability to strike us, must be used to its utmost. It is a mistake to believe that when we win back lost territory we will be able to retrieve and reuse our old transportation, communications, production, and supply facilities that have not been destroyed or crippled, when the enemy withdraws he will leave us only scorched earth and will show no consideration for the welfare of the population.

Therefore, I order 1) All military transportation, communications, industrial and food supplying facilities, as well as all resources within the Reich which the enemy might use either immediately or in the near future to continue the war, must be destroyed. 2) Those responsible for these measures are the military commands for all military objects, including the transportation and communications installations; the gauleiters [district governors] and defence commissioners for all industrial and supply facilities, as well as other resources. When necessary, the troops are to assist the gauleiters and the defence commissioners in carrying out their duties. 3) these orders are to be communicated at once to all troop commanders contrary orders are invalid. (Adolf Hitler 19 March 1945)

Although it did not specify artwork, Göring was convinced that it included their destruction. According to the lootedart website, Adolf Hitler had amassed a large collection of paintings, sculptures, furniture, porcelain, and tapestries that he and his agents purchased or appropriated from confiscated property between the end of the 1930s and 1945. As it was stored in the Führerbau, Munich, while the new Führermuseum was being planned for his hometown of Linz, about 130km north of Bad Aussee, the possibility of an Allied invasion resulted in Hitler ordering what was called the Linz Collection, to be transferred to Altaussee. Reported to be codenamed 'Depot Dora' by Hitler, in May 1944, more than 1,689 paintings arrived at the mine which became the largest repository of looted artwork in Europe. (http://www.lootedart.com/P43P5J761921)

On 29 November 1944, the Control Commission for Germany [British Element] informed the Austrian Control Commission that 'it is reliably reported from Rome railway station that numerous crates of works of art were despatched from there addressed to Franz Hofer, Gauleiter of Tirol and Vorarlberg, Bad Aussee, Austria. These cases were marked 'by personal order of the Fuehrer, the Germany Embassy, Rome'. (TNA FO 1020/2766/3) The rest had arrived by April 1945 when Allied bombing threatened the safety of the artworks stored in six castles and a monastery. (Vaughn, Cy, *Depot Dora: Stolen Masterpieces and Hidden Treasures*, Wheatmark, 2016; Charney, op.cit.)

Gaiswinkler's continued training: October 1944 to February 1945

The impression given by Charney was that Gaiswinkler's American interrogators passed on his intelligence to SOE with the recommendation that, as he knew the area around Alt Aussee, they persuade him to help the Allies rescue the looted art. Although his revelations related to the work of Woolley and the Monuments Men, it is undocumented whether they were given the opportunity to interrogate him or were sent his interrogation report. (Charney, op.cit. p.225)

Gaiswinkler told de Jaeger that he was smuggled across to England and told his interrogators at a house near Reading that, 'according to his miner friends, vast quantities of art treasures were being stacked in the Alt Aussee salt-mines on specially constructed shelves. Many works from the Vienna museums had already been deposited there and new stuff was being secretly brought in all the time. He also told them that he thought Hitler's armies might make a last stand in that corner of the Austrian Alps, no definite information concerning this was available to the Supreme Command of Allied Forces in Europe.' (de Jaeger, op.cit. p.126) Whether Gaiswinkler was referring to Bellasis, Wanborough or another property is unknown, neither is whether he told any of this to Hartog. He claimed that he was asked if he would be 'prepared to go on a sabotage training course and then be dropped in his home area. His task would be to organise local resistance, report on German Army concentration in the area and ascertain what was happening at the salt mines and Töplitzee.' (Ibid, p.127)

Towards the end of October, despite Gaiswinkler needing his eyes tested for practice on the firing range at Stoughton Barracks, Guildford, he was found to be a good shot with both pistol and Sten.

He is inclined to be a little bossy with regard to the other members of the party, but this is possibly due to him having been in charge of the Schutsband [sic] for 2 years, when in Austria. His enlarging of maps and making field sketches are quite good, his work being neat and clearly drawn, (Ibid, 20 October 1944. The Schutzbund was a right-wing anti-communist paramilitary group set up in 1923 by the Austrian Social Democratic Party.)

At the end of October, he was reported to be making progress and maintaining an interest in the work.

When doing route reports and field sketches, his work is always clear and clean. Now, that he has had his glasses, his firing on the range has also improved. He acted as a leader on a scheme [48 – 96 hours practical exercises in a town or city]. His plan was not bad considering it was the first he had to lead. His giving out of orders, however, did not have the required punch and sounded more as if he was giving a lecture. He is inclined to be argumentative which has on several occasions given rise to friction between him and other students. He has not participated in P.T. [Physical Training] this past week owing to his knee giving him some trouble. It is apparently some old trouble, but he had hurt it again when playing basketball. (Ibid. 29 October 1944)

At the end of his training, he was reported to be adequate at weapons; 'still sound if rather dash' at tactics; had 'sounder ideas' of fieldcraft and camouflage; practical and good at map reading; good at demolitions and, despite his bad knee, fit and well in P.T. The general comment was that:

> This man is probably well suited to be a leader as a result of his maturity and background, but he does not inspire confidence when giving orders, nor does he take the trouble to plan his operations carefully. However, if his operation is carefully planned for him, I think he would lead two men as a three-man operation. (Ibid, 1 November 1944)

He had made progress in some areas over the next fortnight, but as regards tactics, it was felt that 'This man will never acquire a steady outlook on a problem. He is slapdash by temperament'. In general, he was considered 'a good man, but is not a really sound man, will always be regarded by his followers as a "bit of a clown". (Ibid, 15 November 1944)

Despite these reservations, SOE persevered with his training, sending him in early December to Ringway Aerodrome (STS 51), what is now Manchester Airport. After being taught how to jump from different heights and land safely, students did practice jumps from a basket attached to an air balloon and then from a hole in the fuselage of a Whitley bomber. To make their practice realistic, one jump was done at night. His knee must have recovered as his instructor commented that:

> This man's age was the only thing against him when he arrived. He was of cheerful disposition and learned the technique well. He appeared to be in a better mental state than the rest of the party and on his first jump he put up an average performance. On his second jump, he slightly sprained an ankle which precluded him from completing the course. There was no hesitation in jumping and with more training might make a reasonably safe risk for his age. (Ibid, 3 December 1944)

Returned to camp, he would have enjoyed his first British Christmas and New Year under what was severe weather conditions for England but probably normal for Austria. He was then sent for clandestine warfare training at Gumley Hall (STS 44), a three-storey mansion with extensive grounds near Market Harborough, Leicestershire. SOE had a policy of keeping students of different nationalities apart. They did not want it known that they were training men who have served in the German armed forces.

At the end of February 1945, Hartog confirmed that there were both Austrians and Germans on the course but only gave the name of one. In his final report on Gaiswinkler, he commented that,

> He is the leader of four Austrians. He is not exceptional, but he is more mature and more stable than the other three and gives them some much-needed weight. He did well on the 48-hour scheme up to a point when things began to go wrong. With the possible exception of Sommer W/T [Wireless Telegraphist] the four of them are such a willing and cheerful crew that it would seem a pity, a really first-class organiser could not go with them: in this case, they would do some really magnificent work. Unlike the Germans, they get on well together and do what they are told. (Ibid, 26 February 1945)

It is worth noting that at that time, Gaiswinkler was not considered first-class. Two days later there was a note stating that he had been attached to the Pioneer Corps with the alias Sergeant Karl Hans Schumacher to cover his journey to 'Maryland'. Once he arrived, he was to revert to his original name.

Maryland was SOE's code name for the German/Austrian Section's headquarters in Bari, a port city on the Puglia coast of Southeast Italy. Following the Allied invasion in September 1943 and the Italians signing an unconditional armistice, SOE transferred staff from 'Massingham', the code name of its headquarters near Algiers, to Bari. SOE in Italy was known as No. 1 Special Force, and it had sections responsible for infiltrating agents to Northern Italy, Greece, Albania, Yugoslavia and Hungary. With so many Allied personnel based there, the German/Austrian Section moved to Monopoli, a small fishing village, about 50 km south. Codenamed ME 43; it was headed by Lieutenant Colonel Peter Wilkinson whose team arranged for agents to be infiltrated into Austria and Germany from Brindisi airfield, about 70km to the south.

By the end of March 1945, as the Allies had pushed the German forces progressively further north, SOE had moved its headquarters from Monopoli to the medieval city of Siena, about 230km north of Rome. (Ibid; Author's communication with Steven Kippax; TNA HS6/22 Maryland 1945)

Alfred Sommer, Operation EBENSBURG's wireless operator

The only other Austrian identified by Hartog in Gaiswinkler's file was Sommer, the wireless operator. There was an Alfred Sommer in the National Archives whose personnel file stated that he was born in Berlin on 12 December 1912, making him 33-years-old. Although his parents were Austrian, he was 'German at birth'. After attending school in Holstein, he worked as a junior clerk in a grocery business at Judendorf Hamburg. Between 1931 and 1933 he worked as a miner at Bergwerk Dortmund, then spent three years with the Haman grocery firm in Neumunster-Heidmuhlen before working for Schramm wine merchants in Schleswig. In 1937 he moved to Austria and worked in a cellulose factory in Fronleiten, Styria, and got married, working for a few months on the Siegfried line and then helping his parents-in-law on their farm. He gave his address as Friesach 3 Post Stubing, Graz.

On 2 February 1941, he was mobilised in the Wehrmacht, the German Army, and served two and a half years as a wireless operator in an artillery unit in Russia before being transferred first to Jersey and then to France. He was interested in fishing and reading and reported that his parents, wife and two of his three children were killed in an air raid at Wiener Neustadt, a city south of Vienna, on 23 August 1943.

At the end of August 1944, as the Germans were retreating in the face of advancing Allied forces, he was captured between Amiens and Beauvais, north-eastern France. Brought to Britain as a prisoner-of-war, there were no details of any interrogation, but he must have convinced his interrogators that he was anti-Nazi as the Commandant at Bellasis reported on 2 October that 'Sommer has now been selected to undergo training at STS 5 [Wanborough].' (TNA HS 9/1390/8)

He was described as 6'1" tall, weighing 176 pounds with light brown, wavy hair; grey eyes; straight nose; square chin;

long face; scar on tip of middle finger, right hand; scar on left shin and left inside thigh. Hartog's first report, almost a fortnight into the assessment, stated that,

> This student was a miner and comes from Graz in Austria. He lived however 18 years un Hamburg, Germany and speaks his German with a Hamburg accent. He is very keen in his work and most attentive, he does not rest until he has thoroughly understood a thing. He is a willing worker and uses his common sense and also can use his hands. He keeps very much reserved from the remainder of the party and usually in the evening retreats to his bedroom early and reads books. He told me, he hopes to go over with 6, 8 and 9 [Gaiswinkler and his team] as they are all Austrians. He also speaks German and does not know English. (Ibid. 14 October 1944)

A week later, his second report added more details about his progress and background.

> This student has had his test for W.T. a couple of days ago. He proved to be able to do 12 words a minute, which is very good considering he has not done any Morse for seven months. He worked as a W.T. operator in the German Army between the regiment and the division. He told me that he was transferred from the Army to the O.T. (Organisation Todt) [German company responsible for the construction of military defences) and was with this organisation for over 1 year. He was working in West Prussia and after that in Dunkirk and St Omer and also in Jersey building fortifications and bunkers of ferro concrete for munitions, stores, etc. His transfer from the Army was indirectly due to his Father who used to drink occasionally rather heavily and who when under the influence of drink, would let steam off, with regard to the Nazi Regime. for this his Father was first placed into the Concentration Camp of Buchenwald, and from there transferred to Dachau. He does not think that his Father is still alive. The Nazis also used to take it out on his family. He was with the Organisation Todt when he was taken prisoner. He has a good physique and is strong as a horse. He is tremendously keen on W.T work and often before breakfast

and immediately after dinner and supper, he works hard to improve his speed. He told me, he soon will get back to his old speed if he only has a little more practice. His drawings and sketches during map reading periods are always neatly done, and his work looks clean. In the making up of [explosive] charges his work is good, it always looks very neat. His shooting is quite good, and he handles the sten and the pistol well. (Ibid, 20 October 1944)

At the end of October, his next report stated that,

He has been working hard during the past week and although things are occasionally a little hard for him, he is a sticker [keeps on with his tasks]. His work for making his route report and sketches is always very good and his drawings are clear and he takes great pains to do his work well. He is however very keen to become a W.T. operator and I have no doubt, that he would be very successful. The only pity with this student is that owing to his nerves, he is very easily irritated by remarks from his fellow students, which leads to slight arguments. The main trouble being that Austrians and Germans don't mix well together, their mentality being so totally different. (Ibid, 29 October 1944)

Sommer's final Training Report at the beginning of November stated that he was fit and tough; an adequate shot; fair at tactics; good at fieldcraft, camouflage and map reading and excellent at demolitions.

A good, tough hard-working soldier, who has now been selected as a Wireless Operator. He should be given a certain amount of "B" training [clandestine warfare] and Map Reading prior to going on operations. He is the most experienced soldier of this group. (Ibid, 1 November 1944)

A fortnight later, it was reported that he was being practised in the tactical handling of his W/T set and map reading. However, he sprained himself during P.T. and had a bad fortnight with his chest. 'Is rather strung up and worried about his health; he is fit to jump, however.' As far as wireless training was concerned, he had satisfied his Sergeant instructor.

Taken to Ringway, he was accommodated at Dunham House, near Altrincham, and on 3 December, it was reported that 'This man arrived here in a very bad state of nerves and considerably run down. He collapsed before any training was started, he should never be asked to jump.' (Ibid. 3 December 1944)

What he and the other Austrians did over Christmas and New Year was undocumented. He was then sent to West Court (STS 6), Finchampstead, Wokingham, Surrey, for specialist wireless training. His instructor's report in early February was not optimistic. 'An extremely neurotic type. He has spent all his time here on wireless training and an opinion of his capabilities cannot be given by us.' The Commandant reported him to be 'Very shy, quiet and retiring, seems to prefer being alone. Physically very strong and a good performer on ropes, though he complains of occasional blacking out. Inclined to become irritable when in difficulties with his W/T set. Does not seem to have the right temperament for W/T work under field conditions.' (Ibid, 12 February 1945)

On 15 February, problems with Operation EBENSBURG were identified. The head of SOE's Group C training schools informed the head of the Austrian Section that Sommer needed a psychiatrist's report before the Training Section would give their consent for him to be sent to Ringway. As the situation had not been resolved, the following week a message was sent to Major Dawson, the assistant head of X Section.

Bonzo Party for Bad Aussee.
Herewith the first snag which will have to be overridden by Higher Authority!

The M.O. [Medical Officer] (I don't know which one) saw Sommer on Friday and said he was so much better he would have no hesitation in letting him jump.

I asked O.C. [Operating Commandant] Group C prior to this to fit him into a course, and he agreed, on the clear understanding that it was Sommer's own wish and irrespective of medical opinion.

Now comes this. The psychiatrist, moreover, is on leave and no one seems to know when he will be back, although he was due today (He is Major Jacobs).

When Major Jacobs has been found and passed a favourable verdict they will then do what they can to get

Sommer up to STS 51, but "the school is very full up with Poles for the next four weeks".
Our target date is to get the party off very early in March, as they ought to go in during the March moon, i.e. latter part of March.
Can ADX [Assistant Head of X Section] come to the rescue, do you think? (Ibid, 21 February 1945)

The psychiatrist must have written a favourable report as arrangements for Sommer's journey to Ringway were sent to the Commandant at Gumley Hall, stating that, 'Sgt. Hartog will report to the School under your command from STS 3 [Stodham Park, Liss, Hampshire] on the morning of Sunday 25 February 1945. He will act as Armed Escort and will conduct the a/m [above mentioned] Student to STS 51. For security reasons, Sgt Hartog should retain the weapon in his pocket and not wear a belt and holster. (Ibid.)

You will provide transport for Sgt Hartog and the Student to Euston Station, so as to arrive there not later than 1700 hours on Sunday, 25 February 1945. On arrival, Sgt Hartog will report to the R.T.O. [Railway Transport Officer] for the purpose of claiming the compartment which has been booked. They will travel on the train leaving Euston 17.40 hours arriving at Wilmslow 21.40 hours.
It is pointed out that the Student should be informed that he is on no account to divulge that he is an ex P.O.W., and should only state, if under pressure, that he is an Austrian and will be infiltrated back into his own Country. This point should be emphasised, as it is anticipated that he will come into contact with a number of "38" Students [Polish].
On conclusion of the Course at STS 51, a compartment will be booked for Sgt Hartog and the Student. They will be met by transport at Euston Station. Sgt Hartog will conduct the Student back to STS 44 [Gumley Hall], and then return to STS 5. (Ibid, 25 February 1945)

Major Dawson reported to Colonel Spooner, who had taken over as head of SOE's Training Section, jokingly telling him that 'he would do his best to find a mud hut or somewhere to put SOMMER for his parachute jumping.' (Ibid. c.25 February 1945)

Sommers was instructed that under no circumstance was he to disclose that he was a prisoner of war but, if questioned, he was allowed to say that he was an Austrian and that he was destined to be infiltrated into his own country. It was stressed that 'to disclose more than this would be 'greatly endangering his own life. A note afterwards stated that 'The fact that this student is not being segregated in no way constitutes a precedent for the training of future Bonzo parties.' (TNA HS8/883, 23 February 1945)

The day before the trip to Ringway, Hartog reported that,

> Of the four Austrians Sommer alone seems to have the heavy over-serious German mentality. But he is undoubtedly most anxious to do a job of work. Conscientious to a fault. Since he has been here, he appears to have become daily more confident and less highly strung though it remains to be seen whether he will survive the ordeal of 51. If he gets through, he should be a useful W/T Operator for the party. (TNA HS 9/1390/8, 26 February 1945)

In the meantime, arrangements for the party's flight to Italy were being prepared. All students would have had to have signed a document saying what should happen if they died on duty. A translation of the uncompleted form reads:

> 'If you receive notice stating that I have died when executing my order, you will endeavour to contact …… after the end of the war. My …… I have supported as far as I know it. They will pay him/her the equivalent in Reichsmark [crossed out and Austrian currency inserted] to the currently prevailing official rates of £ …. Signed …… (Ibid.)
>
> I hereby confirm that the terms of my service have been explained to me and that I agree with the payment in due time:
>
> 1. During my stay in your training and storage facility, I received goods or credit worth 3/- [£0.15] per day from the commander.
>
> 2. As long as I am on duty and actively employed for you according to your instructions, you will credit me with the following: - (a) 3/- per day plus pay (b) 7/- per day for a period

of no more than .... It is agreed that this period is sufficient for the execution of my order.
3. Any amount due to me will be paid out to me at my request in Sterling in Great Britain, otherwise the payment will be made in Austria in Austrian currency if I so wish and the circumstances prevailing at the time allow it.
4. On my return to Great Britain and as long as I stay with you, my salary will endure at 3/- a day. (ibid.)

On 28 February, the Security Section informed the head of the Austrian Section that Sommer had been allocated the name Sergeant Heinz Georg Winter for the trip to Italy. 'His alias is given solely to cover his journey to Maryland where, on arrival, he will revert to his true identity. His cover identity is not given for retention after arrival in Maryland.' (Ibid.)

However, Hartog's report revealed that Sommer's experiences while parachute jumping did not meet expectations. His first jump was from an aircraft at 700 feet with wind speed 6; the second was from 600 feet with wind speed 15.

This student did his ground training very well at 51 and was extremely keen to do his jumps. The first jump was quite good, but on his second jump, he contacted the ground rather heavily. He complained about pains in his back. He was taken to the doctor at Ringway and was sent to the Reception Station at Wimslow where he was X-rayed. The results showed that he has fractured his spine and had to go to the hospital in Chester. He was transferred there on the first of March 45. He is of course very disappointed and hopes that this will not hinder him to be sent on operations. (Ibid, 2 March 1945)

Major Edwards, the Commandant at Ringway, wrote Sommer's Parachute Training report which stated that,

If ever a student tried it was this man. He displayed signs of tension and nervousness throughout the ground training but achieved a good all-round technique. It was a great disappointment to all when he was injured because he had worked so hard and overcome his previous illness and reactions. He showed no hesitation in the aircraft and made a good descent. He was seen to be walking stiffly, and it was suggested that he should see the doctor. This seemed to concern him, and he stated that he was alright and insisted that he was fit to make further descents. He was seen to be waking stiffly after the next descent and was asked to see the doctor. He said he was quite all right, but this time he was taken to see the doctor, and a crushed vertebra was diagnosed. He is a very heavy man and is not fit for his weight. This therefore is against him being a good parachuting risk. TWO DESCENTS NOT CLASSIFIED.

Remarks

All appeared to be going well in the early part of Sommer's training, and the presence of the 38 party with their cheerful attitude towards parachuting has a good effect upon him from the start; they were also very friendly towards him. He was, however, obviously making a great mental effort and suffering under some strain, possibly a fear of a recurrence of his previous "attack". He is keen enough to succeed and suffered bitter disappointment on realising that he was physically damaged after having conquered his nerves. If he is used on operations, I recommend that he relies upon his training he has already received and does not attempt any pure practice jumps. Sgt. Hartog was excellent with him throughout and suffered an equal disappointment. (Ibid. 3 March 1945)

News of his injury resulted in Maryland being sent the following telegram:

W/T OPERATOR OF THIS GROUP HAS INJURED HIS BACK AND CANNOT TRAVEL FOR ABOUT SIX WEEKS.
OTHER THREE MEN LEAVING AS ARRANGED.
CAN YOU POSSIBLY FIND W/T OPERATOR TO JOIN PARTY IN TIME FOR MARCH MOON?
ALTERNATIVELY SUGGEST SENDING IN THE PARTY TO GET THEMSELVES ESTABLISHED AND AWAIT OPERATOR. (Ibid, 1 March 1945)

Sent back to Gumley Hall, there was no sign of his colleagues. They had already left. Sommer must have known his chances of being sent on operations were slight. On 14 March, when the decision was made not to send him to Austria, a telegram was sent to Maryland:

UNFORTUNATELY EDENSBURG W/T OPERATOR WILL NOT BE FIT FOR OPERATION FOR SIX MONTHS. DESIRABLE IF POSSIBLE TO GIVE THEM BONZO OPERATOR FROM YOUR END EVEN IF INFILTRATED LATER.
APPRECIATE THIS MAY NOT BE FEASIBLE AND FAVOUR INFILTRATING PARTY SOONEST IN ANY CASE. (Ibid, 14 March 1945)

When Sommer was informed that he would not be accompanying the EBENSBURG team, he must have been depressed. The Commandant at Bellasis reported that he was 'usually pretty miserable. A radio instructor was due on Thursday or Friday last but has not yet appeared. It will be a good thing when he does. SOMMER told me that he could not stand the plaster of Paris [round his upper body] much longer, and that if he did not get rid of it and go into action in a matter of weeks, he would refuse to do any job later. He worries himself ill, and I cannot say whether this is just wild talk or whether he means it.' (Ibid, 1 April 1945)

When the wireless instructor arrived, he got involved with his training and three weeks later the progress report for '12 Bonzo 7 Sommer' showed that he would have been a competent operator.

> Speed of sending 20/22 wpm – good style
> Speed of receiving 20/22 wpm
> Knowledge of Procedure, "Q" code, knowledge of wireless sets, batteries, aerials, maintenance, etc. very good.
> Working to Signal Plan with STS 52 [Thame Park, Oxfordshire, SOE's Wireless Training Schoool] (six skeds [schedules] per day). Also acting as assistant instructor to 12 Bonzo 39 Kirberg. (About 7 hours W/T per day).
> This student has been much happier during the past week and appears to be losing his fits of depression.
> Does one shooting practice per day with pistol or sten. (Ibid, 15, 21 April 1945)

However, his mood changed and, concerned about his welfare, on 21 May, the Austrian Section sent him to the Military's Cambridge Hospital, Aldershot. Major Griffith's reported that,

> As a complication to his sorrows, he now has had eight teeth out. He remains cheerful and is apparently a good patient but not unnaturally he is considerably worried because he thinks the war will be over before he can be sent to the field. I am afraid this man must be considered a write off for operations, which is a pity when remembering his keenness and [?skill] with wireless. He would like to be allowed to have a small W.T. receiver in hospital to keep up his morse but I doubt if this is possible for security. Is this assumption correct, please? Some more novels in German would be gratefully received.' (Ibid, undated)

When his fracture was healed and his plaster cast removed, he was reported to have been 'very much upset by the news that he was not entirely einsatzfähig [usable], but is now taking his disappointment with fortitude. Is very keen to go into the field and get on with a job. Given a fair break, he might make a success of it, though he is subject to moods and depression if things do not go as well as he hoped. He is very grateful for the books sent. Could some more be sent in about a week's time, please?' (23 April 1945)

By the beginning of May, Sommer was reported to be getting on well and expected to be able to jump again by the middle of September when it was thought it would no longer be necessary. 'He should, however, be very valuable to us in Schleswig-Holstein, where he spent his boyhood and where his real home is with the peasants.' (Ibid. 2 May 1945) Lt Col. Thornley queried whether he should be 'sent back into the PW [prisoner-of-war] stream.' Whether he was sent back to Germany as an agent was undocumented. (Ibid, May 1945)

There was no indication in Gaiswinkler's personnel file how he travelled to Italy nor when, no mention of the other team members who accompanied him on his mission, only that its code name was EBENSBURG. There was no mention of its objectives, no cover story, nor what supplies the team were to be provided with.

The other members of the EBENSBURG team

Gaiswinkler's page on the English Wikipedia website states that 'he was parachuted back into the Aussee area with three colleagues Valentin Tarra: Johann Moser and Hans Renner. This was corroborated by the Special Forces Roll of Honour website which also provided a contemporary photograph and the background found in his personnel file but gives the date of his mission as June 1945, not April. It also stated that they arrived four days before the American forces arrived. As there are no personnel files for any of these men in the National Archives, they could have been aliases.

However, his page on the German Wikipedia website identifies Tarra, Moser and Renner as members of the Austrian resistance, adding that the mission included planning the assassination of Joseph Goebbels, the Reich's minister of propaganda. This was not mentioned in his personnel file. (https://en.wikipedia.org/wiki/Albrecht_Gaiswinkler; https://de.wikipedia.org/wiki/Albrecht_Gaiswinkler; http://www.specialforcesroh.com/gallery.php?do=view_image&id=21608&gal=gallery)

An Internet search revealed nothing on Moser and Renner but the German Wikipedia page identified Gaiswinkler as one of the founding members of the resistance in Bad Aussee in 1940, with Moser, Renner and Tarra, the latter described as a policeman.

It was Charney who identified the rest of Gaiswinkler's team as Josef Grafl, Karl Standhartinger and Karl Schmidt, commenting that although many Austrians had joined the Allies as agents or double agents, 'psychologically, ideologically and physically, these were the cream of the recruits.' (Charney, op.cit. p.225)

Grafl and Standhartinger's personnel files were found in the National Archives but not Schmidt's. It is possible that he had initially been allocated the EBENSBURG mission but was subsequently transferred to another. The issue was partially resolved when an X-Section list of Austrian agents in July 1945 was examined. Karl Schmidt was reported as having been recruited by Count Manfred Czernin, another Austrian SOE agent operating in Italy, but in autumn 1944 he was sent to Villach, a city close to Austria's borders with Italy and Yugoslavia.

Harclerode and Pittaway identified the fourth member of the team as Karl Litzer, aliases Ludwig Roth and Karl Schmidt. (TNA HS6/22, 2 July 1945)

Karl Standhartinger's training October 1944 to February 1945

Standhartinger's file revealed that he was born on 27 March 1920 in Vienna and lived at 10 Landgutgasse 53. Leaving high school in 1934, he worked as a turner in a machine factory and was interested in swimming, cycling and sailing. Recruited into the Luftwaffe in 1941. He was trained to use the telephone and 2cm Vierling anti-aircraft guns. Captured by Canadian troops 25km south of Rouen on 31 August 1944, he was sent to England, presumably to Bellasis. During his interrogation, he must have convinced them that he was anti-Nazi as he was 'put through the cards' on 16 September. When 'no trace' was found against him, the Commandant stated that he had been selected to undergo training at Wanborough on 2 October.

He was described as 5'9" tall, weighing 134lb; blue eyes; light brown hair; round face with a mole on his left cheek; cleanshaven and slim build. Sergeant Hartog's first report stated that,

> This student was of Austrian nationality and comes from Vienna. His age is 23. He is a willing worker and quite enthusiastic and keen. He is attentive during lectures and shows plenty of common sense. He is quite enjoying the course. When in the German army he served in the Luftwaffe. He dislikes the Nazi regime intensely and is longing for the time to see them smashed up. He is not very keen on P.T. and does not like running. He is getting on alright and will shape well as the course proceeds. He has seen service in Russia, France & Holland. He speaks only German with an Austrian accent and does not know any English. (TNA HS9/1404/3, 14 October 1944)

He had provided more background detail in subsequent conversations with Hartog as his next report stated,

> This student has been working well during the past week, he maintains his standard and is shaping well. He seems to be keen on most subjects. He is very keen on sports, and he is a

good player in games such as basketball etc. He told me, in the course of conversation that he has been in Murmansk, Stara Russe, Warsaw and also in France and Holland, while in the German Army. Part of this service he has done with the Flak (Ack Ack) and later served in the Luftwaffe. He is quite a smart fellow and takes things in quickly. He and 7, 8 and 9 get on exceedingly well together, as all four are of Austrian origin. (Ibid, 20 October 1944)

At the end of October, he was reported to be

...doing quite well and progresses satisfactorily, he maintains his keenness and absorbs everything quickly. He is pleasant and cheerful. He puts up with it well having his leg pulled by other students and I have never seen him getting bad tempered. He is looking forward to do his jumping at 51 [Ringway]. He has not yet acted as a leader on a scheme, but he should do quite well. When firing pistol, Sten and the Bren he is amongst the highest score. (Ibid, 29 October 1944).

A fortnight later, he was reported to be a good shot, had learned the basic principles of tactics much better and was good at fieldcraft and camouflage. His map reading was good in practice but he was hindered by a lack of mathematical skills. Like Gaiswinkler, he was good at demolitions. Although he had a bad chest he marched well but was said to be lazy. The general comment was that he was a 'resourceful young soldier, fit for operations in three weeks and for coup-de-mains [surprise attacks].'

His parachute instructor commented at the beginning of December 1944 that,

This man started slowly but picked up the technique reasonably well after a short time. He is young and willing to learn but his nerves seemed to have been affected with the 'horror of jumping' from the remainder of the course. After his first descent, he was a good deal happier and went on to complete the course in good style. He is a fairly safe parachuting risk in good conditions but needs leading the whole time. FOUR DESCENTS SECOND CLASS. (Ibid. 3 December 1944)

Sent to Gumley Hall to continue his training, his report at the end of February suggested that he, 'Has all the Austrian virtues. He is young cheerful and popular. He is not brilliant either physically or mentally. But he will be an asset to the party with his high spirit, and he will give his leader good support.' (Ibid, 26 February 1945)

On the same day, the German/Austrian Section was told that Standhartinger had been given the cover name Corporal Franz Karl Wallner for his journey to Maryland and was to revert to his true identity once there. His alias was Corporal Josef Roth. No details of their briefing with SOE's X Section for Operation EBENSBURG, nor of their journey to Monopoli were included in their files.

Karl Lzicar's training: October 1944 to February 1945

According to Lzicar's personnel file, he was born in Vienna on 25 May 1917 and lived at Dresdenstrasse 64, Vienna XX. The German Wikipedia page identified him as Karl Licca from Vienna. (https://de.wikipedia.org/wiki/Josef_Hans_Grafl) He was described as 5'7½" tall and weighing 165lbs; blue eyes; curly brown hair; Greek nose; heavy face; stocky build with a scar on his left knee.

Both his parents were dead, and he was single. After school, he worked as a mechanic with Fross-Büssing before joining the Austrian Army in 1935 and the Wehrmacht in May 1940. Like Gaiswinkler, he defected while he was in France and lived with the Maquis for four months before reporting to the Civil Affairs Officer in Rouen on 26 September 1944. Sent to Britain, he was interrogated and 'Put through the cards' on 5 October and, when nothing was found against him, he was 'to be trained as an agent commencing 25 October.' (TNA HS9/953/10)

His Wanborough training report a fortnight later stated that he was very keen on weapons training and 'should be a good shot'. He was fair at tactics. 'Has had little experience but should respond quite well.' He was fair at fieldcraft and camouflage but needed more practice. He was good at map reading and had done very well in that subject. He was fair at demolitions: 'Was inclined to be careless at first, but is now improving. He was good at P.T. 'Is very impressive, and at games, has proved to be the best student.' The general

comment was that he 'Should make a good member of a party, but would need a strong leader as he is inclined to be hot-tempered.' (Ibid, 10 November 1944)
Hartog's report a few days later stated that:

This student comes from Vienna and is of Austrian origin. He is 27 years of age. He speaks German with a heavy Austrian accent. While in the Austrian and also while in the German Army he served as a dispatch rider. He has been in Czechoslovakia, Russia and France. He worked with the Maquis in France at Rouen, to whom he had surrendered. He was imprisoned for four months in 1941 for distributing Social Democratic leaflets. He is a willing worker and always polite. When in the Army he had a collision with his motor-cycle, he has scars on his left leg, but this does not trouble him at present, only when marching long distances he quickly gets tired. (Ibid, 13 November 1944)

His second report in early December showed that he had made progress. For P.T. he was described as 'fit, athletic and keen trier. Shows intelligence in combining knowledge with aggressiveness in unarmed combat.' His fieldcraft work had shown 'very fair results.' For weapons training, he was considered 'An Accurate shot with pistol and sten – has produced good results.' He had 'very fair knowledge' of demolitions but 'Needs more practical work to gain confidence. 72% standard in tests.' He had a fair knowledge of map reading and writing reports but needed more practical work. He had good theoretical knowledge of schemes and tactics. 'When leader, issued orders in good sequence but needs more practice to gain confidence. Led his party well.' His general comment was: 'Has worked hard at all subjects and has reached a good average for the party. With more practical Map-Reading and Demolitions he should do well and if he can develop more confidence might show good powers of leadership. (TNA HS9/953/10, 4 December 1944)

Sent to Ringway in December for parachute training, his instructor commented that:

This student seemed quite happy from the start and gave the impression of a quite willing worker. On ground training, he tried hard and developed quite good technique. On his actual jumping, no real nervousness or hesitation was observed although he could not be guaranteed to act quickly and go when ordered unless he was with others of stronger character. FOUR DESCENTS SECOND CLASS. (Ibid, 9 December 1944)

Sent back to Gumley Hall, at the end of February his instructor commented that 'He is as likeable as the other three. He works hard and will do his best in all circumstances. He is not fit for very long marches as his legs trouble him'. (Ibid, 26 February 1945)

Two days later, he was allocated the alias Corporal Joseph Ludwig Roth for his journey to Italy. As none of the other team members' files gave details about the mission objectives, early historians used contemporary Austrian and American sources and made various suggestions which modern historians have questioned. One Maryland file identified EBENSBURG as an 'intelligence mission to contact anti-Nazis in the Salzkammergut area'. Another described it as 'local sabotage' and 'formation of Maquis nucleus.' All 'Bonzos' were told that 'if they worked well they would be remembered after the war, no obligation was incurred.' (TNA HS6/22)

All three men received three shillings (£0.15) a week while in England and told that ten shillings (£0.50) a week would be paid into a British bank account while they were in Austria. They, or their nominated relative, could access the money after the war.

Operation EBENSBURG was one of a number of missions infiltrated into Austria towards the end of the war. Gerald Steinacher's research into SOE's role in Austria revealed that following the German occupation in March 1938 and the arrest of the head of Britain's Intelligence Service in Vienna in August, there had not been enough time to organise an efficient network of agents to support a resistance movement before the war started.

Following the creation of SOE in July 1940, its German and Austrian Section had two objectives. Firstly it was 'to assist in the disintegration of the Third Reich by fostering the soon to be expected all-out revolutionary and separatist uprising in Austria and secondly, to bring about the restoration of Austria as a national unit within the framework of a central European federation.' (Steinacher, Gerald, 'The Special Operations Executive (SOE) in Austria, 1940-1945', *International Journal of*

Intelligence & Counterintelligence, 15, 2002; http://digitalcommons.unl.edu/historyfacpub/140)

Although there was a wide range of small Austrian organisations in London, including the Communist-sponsored Free Austria Movement, the Association of Austrian Social Democrats, the Austria Office, Austrian Academy and the Austrian Centre, they were bitterly divided, and no one group could represent overall opinion in Austria. SOE, therefore, had to follow the Foreign Office's advice to 'limit such informal contacts as prove essential to the bare minimum.' (Ibid.)

Sir George Franckenstein, the former Austrian Ambassador in Britain, concerned that Austria could come under Soviet control, wanted the Allies to promise independence as the way to develop Austrian resistance and encourage them to contribute to the war effort. He also wanted Austrians to be central in encouraging and leading sabotage, revolts and the removal of Austrian units in the Wehrmacht. This promise did not happen until after the Moscow Declaration in November 1943.

Two months earlier, September 1943, the Allies invaded Southern Italy which allowed SOE to send Gerry Holdsworth to set up a forward base in Monopoli. From there, SOE's Central European Section, headed by Peter Wilkinson of SOE's German/Austrian Section, sent 18 missions into Austria and Bill Mathey's SOE office in Bern, neutral Switzerland, sent in 10. (Ibid.)

Although there is a list of SOE operations in Austria on the Wikipedia website, no references are provided, but they are mentioned in five folders of correspondence related to Maryland in the National Archives. (TNA HS6/18-22) Operation DENVER on 8 May 1944 was the first attempt made to contact resistance groups in Sudetenland and establish communications, but all the agents were reported lost through betrayal. Operation CLOWDER in late July 1944 was to make contacts in central and eastern Europe, exploit resistance movements, and look especially to work in Austria and Germany. They only considered the southern parts of Carinthia as 'a realistic base for penetrating Austria.' (Ibid.)

The Slovenian-speaking population living mainly along the Austrian-Slovenian border had already been organised by Josip Broz (Tito) into a few partisan bands. From there, the plan was to penetrate the Austrian heartland but the beginning of 1945 brought total disillusionment. "Clowder" did not consider that the Allies would be able to make "any declaration sufficiently attractive to the Austrians to persuade them to embark on a policy of open resistance, or to help us to any significant extent." A widespread resistance movement was not to be expected before the total defeat of Germany. (Ibid; TNA HS6/17)

Once SOE had been given permission by Bomber Command, 148 Special Duties Squadron began flights from Brindisi and Bari airfields to parachute agents and supplies into the occupied north of Italy and over the Alps into Czechoslovakia and Austria. The BBC broadcast propaganda into Austria but, without military support, the Austrian Resistance could not hope to offer more than passive opposition. In late-March 1945, for example, the BBC's Austrian Service broadcast the following message:

> All become fighters for this Austria, Start acting. Arrange that you put out of action the working of the armament machinery and damage the electric current and gas supplies. You women at home are in so many places in which damage can be done. If each of you daily destroys a piece of machinery, a piece of apparatus, a tool, a connection or a fuse in well-pretended carelessness, or create still greater damage, this will make altogether a big loss for Hitler's mad war, help you to end it and help you to spare the blood of your men. (TNA FO 371 Austria, 22 March 1945)

The British plans for Austria were based on the Moscow Declaration of October 1943 in which In the Foreign Secretaries of US, UK and USSR declared that the Anschluss, annexation of Austria by Germany was null and void and called for the establishment of a free Austria after the victory over Nazi Germany.

> The governments of the United Kingdom, the Soviet Union and the United States of America are agreed that Austria, the first free country to fall a victim to Hitlerite aggression, shall be liberated from German domination.
> They regard the annexation imposed upon Austria by Germany on March 15, 1938, as null and void. They consider themselves as in no way bound by any changes effected in Austria since that date. They declare that they

Operation EBENSBURG

wish to see re-established a free and independent Austria and thereby to open the way for the Austrian people themselves, as well as those neighbouring states which will be faced with similar problems, to find that political and economic security which is the only basis for lasting peace.

Austria is reminded, however, that she has a responsibility, which she cannot evade, for participation in the war on the side of Hitlerite Germany, and that in the final settlement account will inevitably be taken of her own contribution to her liberation. (http://www.ibiblio.org/pha/policy/1943/431000a.html)

It was not until after liberation of France and the retreat of German forces from Italy and Greece in late 1944 that SOE intensified its activities in Austria. As the winter of 1944/1945 was particularly severe, Operation EVANSVILLE did not start until 7 February 1945. This was a mission to provide support for the resistance movement in Graz and make arrangements for agents in Italy but the agent or agents were believed to have been killed and the underground organisation crushed. On 16 February, Operation DUVAL was to contact an underground organisation in Salzburg and assist in sabotage but the team was captured. On 16 March, Operation CROWD was to investigate the general conditions of the underground socialist movement in the Sudetenland, but nothing was heard from the team which was thought to have been captured. On 23 March, Operation ELECTRA was to contact the underground socialist movement in Vienna, but wireless contact was never established. On 2 April, Operation GREENLEAVES was a mission to set up a group at Klagenfurt, but when their documents and photos were captured, the team had to be evacuated to Bari. (https://en.wikipedia.org/wiki/List_of_Special_Operations_Executive_operations#Austria; TNA HS6/18-22)

These setbacks may well explain why, despite his instructors' reservations, SOE decided to send Gaiswinkler as the organiser of Operation EBENSBURG. There was no mention in his file that it was the sabotage mission he claimed when he met the Americans. According to his English Wikipedia page, he was to organise local sabotage with the resistance and capture Bad Aussee. The German Wikipedia page provides much more details.

Joseph Grafl, EBENSBURG's replacement wireless operator

Josef Grafl was Sommer's replacement as the team's wireless operator. According to his German Wikipedia webpage, Gaiswinkler had been recommended a South Tyrolean wireless operator but had turned him down as being a 'black man, politically too close to the middle class'. (https://de.wikipedia.org/wiki/Josef_Hans_Grafl)

Grafl's personnel file in the National Archives provided little biographical information only that he was born on 14 October 1921 in Schattendorf near Eisenstadt and commenced work for SOE as a mechanic on 27 December 1944. His pay was five shillings a day until 8 April, then the same 10 shillings a day while in Austria. He had two aliases, John Green, and Josef Boenisch; the first when he was travelling to Italy and the second while back in Austria. (TNA HS9/606/4)

There was no detail about the intervening years and no evidence of him being sent to Britain for training. However, it did state that he had been engaged by Major Darton to work as the wireless operator for Operation EBENSBURG. SOE's Major James Darton had helped train Soviet agents infiltrated into Europe as part of a secret agreement between Churchill and Stalin, and also worked in Italy with agents destined for Austria. (http://www.iwm.org.uk/collections/item/object/1030014687)

More detail about Grafl's background was provided by Harclerode and Pittaway who interviewed him in 1998.

Coming from a family bitterly opposed to the Nazis, he had been imprisoned prior to the Anschluss for voicing dangerously left-wing sentiments. One of his brothers-in-law was also jailed in 1940 for being a communist. After his release, however, Grafl enlisted in the army and in November 1940 was posted to a specialist radio communications unit, the 1st Funkkompanie, having previously learned how to use a radio while a member of the Socialist Youth Movement near his childhood home in Schattendorf. In the last summer of 1941 he was posted with his unit to take part in the invasion of Russia but after only a few months succeeded in deserting. Using his family's contacts with the Austrian resistance movement, Grafl made his way via the Romanian port of Constanta, through Bulgaria to Greece, where he joined a partisan unit in the port of Piraeus, a short distance from Athens, in the summer of 1942; and it was here that he met SOE agents operating in support of the partisans and arranging supplies of weapons and equipment. (This was not, apparently, the first time that Grafl had encountered members of Britain's clandestine services: in 1939 he had been in contact with two agents, named Miller and Hopson, who had been sent into Austria to gather intelligence on military dispositions within the country.) After several months of involvement in guerrilla operations, Grafl decided to throw in his lot completely with the Allies and was despatched by submarine to Alexandria in northern Egypt. Volunteering for the Royal Air Force, he was subsequently sent to Haifa [STS 102] in Palestine, where he underwent training as a pilot. In early 1945, however, he was transferred to SOE and underwent further training as a wireless operator and a parachutist. (Harclerode and Pittaway, op.cit. p. 103, based on their interview with Grafl on 13 July 1998.)

Like Gaiswinkler, Grafl has a webpage on German Wikipedia, a translation of which reads:

After numerous missions in Asia, however, Grafl had the feeling that he was fighting on the right side but in the wrong place. He asked his superiors to be transferred to Europe to fight for the freedom of Austria. He was then offered to contact the Action Service of the British intelligence service Special Operations Executive, as he could count on at least operations near his home there. Unaware of what kind of missions this would be, Grafl accepted this offer in 1944 and was initially trained under the code name "Josef Green" in Hong Kong as an agent and introduced in various sabotage techniques. The British secret service had begun at this time, in close coordination with the Enlightenment [sic. Intelligence Service], to parachute special forces behind the German lines by parachute to prepare for the advance of the Allies in enemy territory with the help of sabotage. Grafl participated in a total of 34 parachute operations in which bridges were blown up, and the German retreat sabotaged. As a result, he earned the reputation among the British to be an experienced warhorse and therefore the intelligence service also resorted to him, as a special operation was planned on Austrian soil. (https://de.wikipedia.org/wiki/Josef_Hans_Grafl)

Research by historian Dr Peter Pirker revealed that Grafl had several times mentioned a British officer named 'Captain Miller'. From the name and personal descriptions, Pirker identified him as Hans Müller, a 55-year-old German businessman, also known as Herbert Miller. In 1943/44, as a civilian in Serbia, he cooperated closely with the SOE mission that supported Cetnik leader Mihailovic. At the end of May 1944, Miller was flown out to Bari. SOE's X Section in Monopoli used him from the end of August 1944, especially for recruiting in POW camps. Sent to Egypt, he interviewed Austrians in the POW camp and recruited a group, including Grafl, which was brought to Monolopi at the end of January 1945. (Pirker, Peter, '*Subversion deutscher Herrschaft Der britische Kriegsgeheimdienst SOE und Österreich*', Vienna University Press, 2012, pp.239-40)

SOE had two paramilitary training schools near Brindisi, one in the 'liberated' Castello di Santo Stefano, a few kilometres south of Monopoli, and another in unfinished sanatorium buildings at Ostuni, an inland town about 30km south of Monopoli. They had a parachute training school at San Vito del Normanni, near Brindisi airfield. and a wireless training school in Villa Chiocciola. (Valentine, I. (2006), *Station 43: Audley End House and SOE's Polish Section*, Sutton Publishing, p.121; Author's communication with Steven Kippax)

When the other three members of the EBENSBURG team arrived in Italy was undocumented in their personnel files, nor what happened to them subsequently apart from a summary of their mission provided by Lieutenant Colonel C.H. Villiers of the Grenadier Guards. After Germany surrendered in July 1945, he was sent out to Maryland to arrange the discharge of the Austrian Bonzos. These summaries are referred to later.

According to Harclerode and Pittaway who accessed 148 Squadron records and interviewed Grafl, they were flown to Maryland on 28 February. Gaiswinkler claimed he had to use the name Major Thomas. (Harclerode and Pittaway, op.cit. p.114)

The EBENSBURG team in 'Maryland' February to April 1944

When the Supreme Headquarters of the Allied Expeditionary Forces (SHAEF) was informed that there were a number of prisoners of war camps in Austria, for fear of German reprisals, they proposed to forbid the supply of arms and ammunition to nearby resistance groups. On 26 March, one of the X Section officers, codenamed X/A.2, wrote to Lt Col Ronald Thornley, the assistant director, codenamed AD/X.1, commenting that:

> I fail to see how SOE could operate at all. If all arms and ammunition, with the exception of personal weapons for agents, are banned, how can we equip the small groups which we still live in (vain?) hope of forming. Similarly, if we cannot drop sabotage material within 25 miles of any known PoW Camp in AUSTRIA, it excludes nearly all the areas where we have already dropped parties and are planning to drop many more. In fact, it is difficult to know where one could drop anybody except in the extreme West of AUSTRIA. This ban would certainly rule out EBENSBURG who are standing by now, as I understand that a small PoW camp is situated quite near their dropping point.
> I will certainly instruct all our parties to keep clear of PoW, but hope the rest of SHAEF's instructions are due to a momentary panic. As you say, if the GERMANS want a pretext for the massacre of PoW, they will find one in any case, so it seems stupid to be so careful as to hamper our whole course of action. If any further instructions are issued by SHAEF, I should very much like to hear them. Meanwhile, I shall continue to be very cautious, but otherwise, the most sensible thing seems to be to wait for orders from AFHQ [Allied Forces Headquarters]. Under whose wing it is occasionally very convenient to shelter. Do you agree? (TNA HS6/20, 26 March 1945)

On the same day, 26 March, X/Aus.1 received a letter from X/A.3.

> I have had a really hectic time with EBENSBURG, first

of all finding a W/T operator about 4 hours before the whole lot of them moved up to Siena, then preparing all his documents and getting his kit. All of which was complicated to the nth degree by the fact that the bulk of our stores had already gone north and we had none of the [German] uniforms etc. down here. Why orders were given by Sgt M to move in the middle of a moon period just when drops were really starting again I can't imagine – nor can anyone else. It couldn't have come at a more inopportune moment. Then the RAF dug their toes in and said they were not going to move north, and now eventually we are being given an American Wing for our ops, just as we have at last established a really good liaison with the Wing here. We are none of us very keen on American pilots, but we hear that this Wing is pretty good. Let's hope it proves so. You will be interested to hear that last night when Eveleth [another Bonzo agent] there was a very funny scene at the aerodrome. There stood the little man in is German uniform being made a great fuss of by the crew, who all said he looked so young, and finally the Squadron Leader said he would like to pilot him himself and did so! And little Eveleth who spoke not one word of English just beamed on them all, was perfectly calm and just did everything he was told with a smile. We are hoping to get EBENSBURG off tomorrow; it's been rather a business getting them ready as somehow some of their kit must have gone astray in the packing room. Alex R. brought out the 6 kitbags, but one man had no shirts, another no socks and so on, and all our stores had gone north!! [SOE had buildings at Ampugnano (ME 102), near Siena]. Also some of their papers were not quite as they wanted them; they put it down to the fact that the officer who interviewed them did not speak much German (that was their account – I don't know who it was, perhaps they spoke too broad Austrian) but we have managed to make the necessary alterations, and all is now in order. Jimmy and our secretary and most of the Office papers went up early this week, leaving me here as the rear party, together with Althea and our Liaison officer with the RAF, and we shall stay till all operations scheduled for this moon have got off. But I can't tell you how complicated it is especially as [telegraph] signals take days to get here, the telephone is far from good, and it takes 3 days by road for

Operation EBENSBURG

anything else to get up there.

[...] I am not looking forward at all to going up to Siena. It will be far too crowded and in a small space like that you can't get away from the people. Then all of us, No. 1, Force 139 and SOM will be herded together in one large building, and the moment you have an organisation like that, the whole thing is changed. However, I am hoping it won't be for too long and that we shall moved into the promised land soon.

By the way, I think one episode this morning might amuse you. I had everything ready for the EBENSBURG W/T operator, with the exception of a German army belt. I had begged, borrowed but not stolen the rest of his uniform – ours all being up north – but nobody could produce a belt. All the other organisations were most helpful and tried their hardest but there was no belt to be had, and they were due to go in tomorrow. I had sent one of the Greenleaves party down to a P/W camp where he had been working for PWB to try to get one, but he reported nothing doing. So this morning I took the P.U. and went there myself, armed with a tin of 50 cigarettes. I have been there at various times and they all know me quite well by now. I was received with a terrific salute by the sentry at the gate and was escorted along to the Commandant's office, all the ORs [Ordinary Ranks] saluting with great empressement [eagerness] while the Prisoners behind the barbed wire all goggled at me. I confided to one of the captains in the office what I wanted, and he said I must have it by hook or by crook if necessary and produced my tin of cigarettes as a bait. He called a conclave of one or two officers and a couple of NCOs [Non-Commissioned Officers], and finally, one of them went away with the tin of cigarettes, and in five minutes my belt appeared!! I walked back to the gate in triumph again being saluted all the way and returning it of course while the prisoners still goggled behind the barbed wire. It was as good a play. But I got my belt, all highly irregular of course, but what's the good of being in SOE if you can't do something like sometimes. (Ibid, 25 March 1945)

In Wilkinson's correspondence to Dawson, dated 5 April 1945, he mentioned that,

As far as Joes generally are concerned, the limiting factor is W/T operators, as although we have an adequate number of Bonzos under training, they will not be ready, with a few exceptions, until mid-April. In principle, I have told X/A2 that absolutely, as soon as any party is ready it should be bunged in [infiltrated]– because in the present disorganisation in Austria the risk is negligible – and there is no time for preparing too detailed documents and cover stories and no need either. [...]

The para-mil[itary] parties are all due for 'bungers'. I really feel that can be useful in creating confusion, and only hope we can get them off in time. They arrive here from the South tomorrow, and we will put them on high priority and try and cajole the Air Force into agreeing a non-moon bunger. If need be. Because time is growing desperately short.

If the various, most of these are held up for want of a W/T, but as soon as the latter is ready, then bungers for them too. (Bungers, need I say, is MXA's expression). (TNA HS6/20, 5 April 1945)

The EBENSBURG team's Operation Order was not found in the Maryland files but to give one an idea of what it would have looked like, the Operation Order for the CROXTON mission, flown out three weeks later, is included., Gainswinkler would have been given one headed EBENSBURG.

TOP SECRET
INFORMATION
1.(a) General Information
Our immediate aim in AUSTRIA is to prepare the way for a full implementation of the MOSCOW Declaration at a later date. The following points are important:
We must sever military, political and economic connections with GERMANY immediately and liberate AUSTRIA from German domination.
We must ensure execution of the surrender terms.
We must make available to the United Nations all Austrian economic resources not required for the civil population.
We must facilitate the transfer of control from the present

Nazi administration to Allied Military Government. This will lead through various stages to the final establishment of a free and independent AUSTRIA.

During the period of Allied Military Government, no local personalities or organised political groups will be allowed to determine (or to think that they determine) policy, and no commitment will be made to any political group although their views and opinions will be welcomed.

We shall establish freedom of worship, speech and meeting, but no public elections for some considerable time.

Pending the decisions of the Peace Conference, the Austrian frontier will be re-established provisionally as on 31 December 1937.

Information about the Enemy (For Croxton)
(Map reference)
General Disposition and Intention

There are indications that the enemy is planning a withdrawal into the mountains of the Salzkammergut, Tirol and Vorarlberg. The boundaries of this so-called "Inner Festung" are at present unknown, but it is possible that the Wörgl/Kitzbühel area is inside these boundaries.

Order of Battle in your area

In view of the rapidly changing situation, it is impossible to give accurate information about the movement of troops in the area, and only the locations of the following units are available:

873 Landesstûrm Bn. Innsbruck
940 Landesstûrm Bn. Sea Feld.
88 Pionier Regt. Detachments throughout Tirol.
124 Pionier Regt. Detachments throughout Tirol.
27 Pionier Bn. Innsbruck.

Information about own troops

Map reference: Sheets ...

Russians. The main Russian drive has so far been directed towards Linz and the North West. After the capture of Linz it is very probable that the attack will be continued in the direction of Salzburg and Berchtesgaden, but it it is not anticipated that Russian troops will occupy the Kitzbühel/ Wörgl area. In view of the advances of the American 3rd Army, it is possible that the Russians and Americans will meet in the Linz area.

15. A.2

Americans. The latest advance of the 3rd Army is in the direction of Passau and it seems probable that troops will cross the Austrian frontier in the very near future. Further units of the 3rd and 7th Armies are advancing towards Munich where resistance is expected to be stiffer. It is reasonable to suppose that these will be the troops to reach the Wörgl area first.

Partisan and Patriot Forces

Armed bands of deserters from the Wehrmacht and foreign workers are known to be operating in the mountains of the Tirol and the Inn Valley.

Ground

You should study the following: -

Maps

Air photos

INTENTION

Your main task, which you will make every effort to carry out, is included in Annex B. At the same time you will endeavour to carry out the following secondary tasks: -

Harassing the German retreat.

Spreading of Rumours likely to lower morale and cause disorganisation in the German Army

Inciting members of the Wehrmacht to desert.

Assisting Allied POWs, so long as this does not prejudice your principle tasks.

Reporting troop and supply movements, identifications of Units, dumps, A.A. posts, aerodromes and other military intelligence.

Reporting German plans for sabotage, subversive or guerrilla action after the Allied occupation.

Reporting news of other Allied agents which you receive. In the event of a surrender or of a collapse of German resistance you will: -

Instruct Allied POWs to stay where they are till the Allies arrive.

Persuade local inhabitants to look after Allied POWs until the Allied Armies arrive.

Prevent destruction of public utilities by the Germans – bridges, factories, gas and water works, banks and post offices, etc.

Cooperate with Allied Military Government officers on their arrival.

Operation EBENSBURG

Use your influence to prevent civil war and excesses by the populace, and more especially by Partisan elements.
You will not repeat not at any time: -
Arm Allied POWs.
Attempt to form large resistance movement.
Discuss surrender with any German Commander except on unconditional terms. You will report all such approaches immediately to Headquarters.
In the event of your being overrun by Soviet troops, you will report to the nearest Unit and declare yourself to be British Officers (or O.R.s [Ordinary Ranks]) if in uniform and British agents if in civilian clothes.

METHOD
6. Your party consists of: -
7. Your party will deplane in order as detailed by Leader and on dropping will carry out drill laid down by him for the location of other members and stores.
8. The Drop
(a) Area...
Latitude
Longitude
(b) Date
(c) Time

ADMINISTRATION
9. Cash Allotment: Gold
　　　　　　　　　Dollars
　　　　　　　　　RM
　　　　　　　　　Lire
　　　　　　　　　Various

Details of personal arrangements will be handed into H.Q. or made directly with the Finance Officer or Camp Commandant.

Mail: All personal mail will be sent to Head Censor, No. 6 Base Censor Group, C.M.F. [Central Mediterranean Forces], whence it will be forwarded to this H.Q. and held here until the opportunity arises for its onward despatch. If periodical letters are to be sent to relatives by H.Q., details will be handed in before departure.

Stores: Your party will take the following: (This is what one party was allocated)
　　　200 rounds Beretta ammo

2 lightweight sleeping bags
3 pairs mountaineering boots
3 combination knives
3 .32 automatics
150 rounds ammo
6 torch batteries
3 shoulder holsters
6 ankle supports
3000 cigarettes
Matches
Tobacco
Pepper
Master keys (Dietrich)
Razor blades
Shaving soap
Pistol cleaning rods, brushes, etc.
Writing pad
Cases for binoculars
Bottle whiskey or rum

INTERCOMMUNICATION

10. You will have the following signal equipment which will be the responsibility of….
   A Mk. II WT set. 2
   Hand generator (Hoover)
   Batteries 6.V. 40. 2
   Aerial camouflage
   Voltmeter
   Operating lamp 6 or 6a.
   Pliers side-cutting 5"
   Clothes line aerial
   WT Key 8 amp
   Vibrator

You will work Signal Plan … (CROXTON/YELLOW) direct to Headquarters and you should make contact as soon as possible on arrival.

IMPORTANT

11. You will destroy this Operation Order when memorised in the presence of the Officer who delivers it to you.
12. You will submit to headquarters in writing a copy of your Operating Orders to other members of your party within 4 hours of receipt of this paper. (TNA HS6/21, 25 April 1945)

Operation EBENSBURG

By spring 1945, SOE's belief that an Austrian resistance could help in the liberation of their country had become a reality. The EBENSBURG team would have been briefed on their mission by Wilkinson or other X Section officers and final preparations made. An SOE liaison officer would have negotiated with the RAF for a plane to drop the agents with their containers during the nights of the full moon. For agents infiltrated or exfiltrated by sea, the Royal Navy needed to supply motorboats or submarines. (Email communication with Steven Kippax)

According to Harclerode and Pittaway, their primary mission was to investigate and report on the situation at the mine repository. Their secondary mission was to organise the local resistance and gather intelligence about the locations and deployments of Wehrmacht formations and units. This included the area around Töplitzee. However, these were not mentioned in their personnel files nor in the Maryland correspondence.

They would have been shown maps and aerial photographs of their drop zone and provided with details of the current situation 'in the field', the expression used for being in occupied territory. SOE agents already operating in Austria were in wireless communication with Bari. SOE and MI6 was collecting intelligence in Bern, Switzerland and the code-breakers at Bletchley Park were listening in and decrypting German communications. From these intelligence reports it is likely that the EBENSBURG team were informed that General Fabianku's Sixth Army had been ordered to withdraw from the Balkans to defend the Nazis' 'Alpenfestung' (alpine fortress) near Bad Aussee. Officers of the Schutzstaffel (SS), Hitler's 'Protection Squadron', and Sicherheitdienst (SD), the SS and Nazi Party's intelligence agency, were conducting court martials and executing anyone suspected of anti-Nazi sympathies or activities. There were also German troops crossing the Pötschen Pass towards Salzburg and Germany having retreated from Greece and Yugoslavia. Counter Intelligence reports based on interrogations of captured Abwehr, SS and other officers suggested the Germans were fearful of being caught by the Russians, preferring to surrender to the Americans. Many officers had been ordered to report to their units who had retreated to Bavaria and Austria but went AWOL instead, hiding in remote Alm farms, where there was plenty to eat, and berghutten, mountain huts. There was the belief that the Nazis would make their last stand in Austria. Many Nazi refugees were billeted with families in Bad Aussee. The family of SS Obersturmbannführer Adolf Eichmann, the organiser of the Holocaust, was living in Altausse. De Jaeger reported that the German Foreign Office had been evacuated to villas in the Bad Aussee area along with the puppet governments of Serbia, Croatia, Hungary and Bulgaria, with their gold reserves and foreign currencies. (de Jaeger, op.cit. p.127; email communication with Dr Adrian O'Sullivan FRHistS and Steve Tyas; http://oesterreichterrorismus.blogspot.com/ 2014/08/kriegsverbrecherjagd-im-ausseerland.html)

To ensure the men's safe arrival, a reception committee made up of members of the local resistance group would have been told the date and expected time of their drop and who would help collect and store their four containers of supplies and take the agents to safe houses.

The flight to Austria: 8 April 1945

Taken to Brindisi airfield during the mid-March moon period, they were put on a plane, but bad weather caused the pilot to abort the mission and return with the passengers and containers. De Jaeger, who interviewed Gaiswinkler after the war, reported a second flight having to be aborted for the same reason. (Harclerode and Pittaway, op.cit. p.104; de Jaeger, op.cit. p.126)

There was a delay until the start of the next moon period in early April. Taken from Bari to Brindisi airfield in a closed truck at dusk, the driver drove straight to the waiting Halifax, 'T for Tommy', and reversed so that there was little chance of anyone else on the airfield seeing them board the plane. According to the 148 Squadron records, the plane took off at 23.45 on 8 April with no clouds and a full moon. After following the east coast past Ancona, they turned north between Venice and Trieste and headed towards Austria. (TNA AIR 27/996 148 (SD) Squadron Record of Operations Book, January 1944 – May 1945)

Bill Leckie, the pilot, and Flight Sergeant John Lennox, the despatcher, who had both been on several previous missions to drop agents and supplies, reported to Harclerode and Pittaway that the inside of the fuselage was unheated so the passengers would have been cold and stiff. At 02.50, half an hour before the

Operation EBENSBURG

drop, they were told to get ready.

'Under their parachutists' helmets and jumpsuits, they wore civilian clothes and boots suitable for the mountainous terrain over which they would have to make their way. Each was armed with a Beretta 7.65mm calibre pistol and fighting knife carried in the pockets in their jumpsuits. Their other weapons and equipment, including Josef Grafl's high-frequency transmitter/receiver, were in four containers carried in the aircraft's bomb-bay.

When all four had checked their personal equipment and pronounced themselves ready, Flight Sergeant Lennox led them towards the tail of the aircraft where he positioned them sitting in pairs by the trapdoor covering the large circular aperture in the floor through which they would make their exit. Lennox clipped the end of the static line of each man's parachute to a D-ring set in the port side of the fuselage. Shortly afterwards the Halifax banked gently and began the first of two flights over the dropping zone at an altitude of 800 feet. The bomb aimer, Flight Sergeant Brian Douglas, opened the doors of the bomb bay containing the team's four containers; minutes later, he released the containers, and the aircraft flew on in a wide circle. From his turret in the tail the rear gunner Flight Sergeant Charlie Leslie, watched the four container parachutes floating earthwards. At this point, Flight Sergeant Lennox opened the trapdoor covering the aperture, and a loud blast of cold air and noise filled the aircraft interior.

As the aircraft began to line up for the second approach, the four men readied themselves for the jump. When the command to drop came through Lennox's headset and the green light came on, he shouted 'Go!', tapping Gaiswinkler and Grafl on the shoulder. As the two men dropped down through the aperture, Lennox gave a thumbs-up signal to Standhartinger and Litzer [sic], who followed immediately. As each man fell away from the aircraft, his parachute was extracted from its pack by its static line, and all four were soon descending towards the dark mountainside below.

A strong wind caused the parachutes to drift rapidly away from the centre of the drop zone; nevertheless, Gaiswinkler and his companions all landed safely and, having buried their parachutes in the deep snow, regrouped. There was, however, no sign of the expected Resistance reception committee, or of the four equipment containers. (Harclerode and Pittaway, op.cit. pp.104-5 based on their telephone interview with John Lennox, 6 August 1998)

Charney reported that, at that time, Leckie had 'absolutely no previous idea' of the men's mission.

Security at that time was 100% efficient, with no indication of what was about to take place, other than fulfilling our own particular task to the best of our ability. As pilot and captain of a Halifax aircraft about to embark on an SD [Special Duties] operation, I was fully briefed with the exception of... learning any details about the four persons we had been instructed to drop over our specific dropping zone. To ensure maximum security in line with Special Duties practice, there was no communication between aircrew and the SOE agents, other than the dispatcher making them familiar with dropping procedures. (Charney op.cit. pp.228-9)

The EBENSBURG team's arrival and first weeks in Austria

Grafl reported the drop after the war. 'It was terrifying. It was dark, and there was snow, plenty of snow. I landed in a drift which came up to my shoulders. I lost my emergency kit. On top of this, it was my first time in the mountains. But I realised that there might be situations like this. When I was asked by a British officer to parachute, I said all right because I thought I would jump and then go home.' (Harclerode and Pittaway, op.cit. p.105; interview with Josef Grafl, 13 July 1998)

Only one of the containers was found, the one containing Grafl's wireless set. According to Gaiswinkler, it had been so badly damaged on impact; it was irreparable leaving the team with no contact with Bari. This was disputed by Grafl who claimed that, as it was too heavy to carry down the mountainside, he persuaded Gaiswinkler to leave it buried in the snow. (https://de.wikipedia.org/wiki/Albrecht_Gaiswinkler)

When it became light enough to see, it was realised that they had been dropped in the wrong place, several kilometres from the planned drop zone. Their map reading and orienteering skills came in useful. Gaiswinkler determined that they had come down on the Höllingebirge instead of the Zielgebeit am Zinken plateau, about 40km from Bad Aussee. Just below them was the mountain town of Feuerkogel and the area's most notorious prison camp at Ebensee.

Leckie explained to Harclerode and Pittaway that 'It was the only occasion on which we dropped four "Joes", as we called our passengers; we normally carried only one or two plus their containers. The weather was fine, otherwise the drop would not have taken place, and I remember clearly seeing the lights of villages in the valleys below.' (Ibid, p.106) He disagreed that they had been dropped in the wrong place, claiming that they had been dropped 'blind', with no reception committee. 'We would have been briefed beforehand on whether or not there would be a reception committee. If there was to be one, we would have been told the pre-arranged pattern in which the flares would be laid out on the DZ and the code latter which would be flashed at us by a torch from the ground. If the flare pattern or code letter was not correct, or if we could not see any, I would have aborted the drop. On the other hand, if we had been told the team was jumping blind, with no-one down below to meet them, we would have dropped them accordingly. In this instance, where there was no one on the ground, we must have been told that they were jumping blind otherwise we would not have dropped them.' (Ibid.)

Harclerode and Pittaway suggested that as SOE had captured German-trained Italian agents who reported being sent to investigate sabotage training camps in Bari and Monopoli in early 1945, there were concerns that there might be double agents in their headquarters and amongst the Austrian Resistance and so decided to send the team in blind. (Harclerode and Pittaway, op.cit. p.106; TNA WO204.11987, 23 December 1944)

As well as not being able to locate their containers, there was the added stress of hearing the approach of men and dogs up the mountain tracks. Having been warned in Bari of garrisons of German troops in the area, they suspected they had heard the aircraft and, suspecting parachutists had been despatched, had sent out patrols. With nowhere for them to hide on the bare, snow and ice-covered mountainside, they removed the contents of their only container and buried it in the snow with their parachutes, harnesses and jumpsuits. To evade capture, they avoided the tracks and mountain paths and made their way down through the pine forest to Steinkogl bei Ebensee. According to Grafl, 'We went directly to the town's railway station and went by train to Bad Aussee. We heard rumours about the Englishmen who had landed.' (Ibid, p.107) Using the skills learned during their SOE training at Wanborough, they avoided any possible control points at Bad Aussee by jumping off the train before it reached the station.

Making contact with Gaiswinkler's brother, Max, he was informed about the strength of local resistance. Despite the great risk to himself and his family, Max provided temporary accommodation. As other villagers had been told that Gaiswinklert was a prisoner-of-war, it was imperative he should never be seen in public. Later, a shed in the woods above the village was used as a base and children of the resistance members took them food and other supplies. Gaiswinkler went down at night to his father's house where, through Max, he held meetings with the Resistance leaders.

Sepp Plieseis, the communist leader of the 'Willy-Fred' group of about 30 men, was reported to have been unenthusiastic about engaging in open combat. He had fought in the Spanish Civil War, been interned in France, captured after he escaped and sent by the Germans to Linz prison. Refusing to join the Wehrmacht, he was sent to Dacahu concentration camp, from where he escaped and was hiding out in the Salzkammergut mountains. His principal aim was to provide sanctuary for deserters. However, he contacted the eighty workers at the mine and formed a sub-group led by Mark Pressl and Alois Raudaschl. (https://de.wikipedia.org/wiki/Sepp_Plieseis)

Valentin Tarra, Gaiswinkler's old comrade from 1940 who was the head of a resistance group around Bad Aussee, was more cooperative. Until Gaiswinkler team's arrival, his group had been ineffective as it only operated in small cells and had no coordination. Several members of his group had been killed in an air raid in the Autumn of 1944 and others betrayed to the Gestapo by a Ukrainian informer. With the help of Tarra, Gaiwinkler persuaded the members of the local mountain rescue team and the town's gendarmerie to support him. The latter assisted with weapons, ammunition, vehicles and equipment. Harclerode and Pittaway, op.cit.)

Operation EBENSBURG

Three days after the EBENSBURG party had been dropped, 11 April, X/Aus.1 reported to X/A.3:

I cannot tell you how pleased we are, and in particular I am, that you got a W/T Operator into the EBENSBURG team and got them off. I know you would have been impressed by the genuine, stalwart qualities of the three chaps we sent you, and it was a great feat to get them right into the Redoubt (now known as Schlupfwinkel) just at this moment.

I do not understand why EBENSBURG's kit did not reach you properly, but possibly the missing articles left here earlier by bag and fetched up too late to be of any use. You cannot imagine what uphill work it is to achieve the ordinary, mundane success of despatching you an urgent parcel. We are at present being worn to a frazzle to get off your stop-press things [15 pay books] this week! Nobody's fault and doubtless very good for our tempers! (I only put this remark in to show you that when things do not arrive in that apple-pie order we should like them to, it does not mean slackness or half-heartedness at this end.)

[...] Incidentally, the Colonel said I was to be sure to give you a pat on the back for getting the chaps off so well. (TNA HS6/22, 11 April 1945)

Analysis of reconnaissance photographs of the Salzkammergut area, southeast of Salzburg, showed new roads, bunkers, ammunition and store dumps. This led the OSS, the Office of Strategic Services, the United States' equivalent of SOE, to believe that this was the 'National Redoubt, where the eltite Nazi troops would finally retreat to and descend 'to prey like werewolves on the Allied occupation forces'. The 80th Infantry Division was ordered back from Russia in early May 1945 not only to harass the retreating forces of General Sepp Dietrich's Sixth SS Panzer Army but also to counteract the threat of the SS's National Redoubt. (https://www.cia.gov/library/center-for-the-study-of-intelligence/kent-csi/vol4no2/html/v04i2a07p_0001.htm)

Gaiswinkler learned that the reports of an alpine fortress where the Nazis would have their last stand had been a German propaganda lie but was unable to pass on this intelligence to the Allies without a wireless set.

61

Tarra put Gaiswinkler in contact with sympathetic salt miners at Altaussee and the two men in charge of the artworks in the mine, Professor Michel and Karl Sieber, who was responsible for restoration work. Unknown to the Germans, Michel liaised with the Resistance and was reported to have been a secret communist. Having contact with Emmerich Pöchmüller, the mine's General Director, Michel was able to provide Gaiswinkler with information about the mine and the presence of Germans in the area. Within three weeks, according to an SOE report, he had built up a group of 360 men although this number was disputed by Grafl. (TNA HS7/146; de Jaeger, op.cit. p.130; Harclerode and Pittaway's interview with Walter Tarra, 14 July 1998; Charney, op.cit. p.247; http://www.ooegeschichte.at/epochen/oberoesterreich-in-der-zeit-des-nationalsozialismus/widerstand/widerstandsgruppen/widerstand-im-ausseergebiet.html)

British intelligence had reported Goebbels as being on holiday at Villa Castiglione, a large property on the banks of Grundlsee, near Bad Aussee. However, when it was learned that he had left for Berlin two days before they arrived and unable to contact Bari, the arrest or assassination mission was aborted. (Charney, op.cit. pp.225-6; https://de.wikipedia.org/wiki/Albrecht_Gaiswinkler)

The villa, where much of Hitler's Linz Collection was stored, was taken over by Oberstgruppenführer Ernst Kaltenbrunner, the Austrian Chief of the Reichsicherheithauptamt (Reich Central Security Office) where he set up his headquarters. On 18 April 1945, Reichsführer Heinrich Himmler, the Head of the SS, appointed Kaltenbrunner head of the remaining German forces in Southern Europe. His communications with Hitler and the German High Command were from a wireless transmitting station in Kerry Villa, situated on top of a hill near Altaussee.

In order for Grafl to establish contact with X Section in Bari, he needed a receiver/transmitter. The only option was to 'acquire' one of the German sets. Through Tarra, an approach was made to someone he knew who was working at Kaltenbrunner's headquarters. Supplied with a 'spare' set, Grafl was then able to establish contact with Bari, report on the situation and receive orders. What is undocumented is whether Gaiswinkler's men were able to retrieve the missing containers and whether SOE arranged to send in replacement supplies.

A group was ordered to set up a camp in the woods near

Operation EBENSBURG

the mine to keep watch and report on any developments. Miners were provided with weapons and similarly reported back on what was happening.

Another German officer who had moved with his family to one of the villas in Bad Aussee in March 1945 was Wilhelm Hoettl who worked in the foreign section of the SD. Based in Budapest in 1944, daily reports from the SS headquarters, the Hungarian Ministry of War and a conversation with Eichmann, convinced him that the Reich had no future. Contacting Allen Dulles, the representative of the OSS in Bern, he agreed to work for the Americans and, learning that the Allies planned to divide Austria into four zones and that Vienna would be in the Russian zone, he decided to move to the American zone. Whether Dulles or Bari HQ informed Gaiswinkler that Hoettl would be a useful contact is unknown. Hoettl admitted to de Jaeger that he met Gaiswinkler at his hideout. As he worked at Kerry Villa, Hoettl was able to supply Gaiswinkler with intelligence and pass on Gaiswinkler's message to Dulles to request the Americans not bomb the Bad Aussee area. Whether this was after a request from Bari or whether he acted independently is unknown. (de Jaeger, op.cit. p.134; Harclerode and Pittaway, op.cit. p. 109-10)

Following the American forces invading Southern France in August 1944, German forces were being pushed back into Germany. In late 1944 they began retreating from Greece fearing that the advancing Russian army would cut them off.

On 29 March 1945, Captain Robert K. Posey, one of the Monuments Men, was serendipitously introduced to Bunjes in a village outside Trier, near the Luxembourg border. Suffering from toothache, he visited the local dentist. Following a conversation about what work he was doing, the dentist introduced Posey to his son-in-law, whose home was decorated with what looked like well-known works of art.

Fearing revenge from the Nazis, Bunjes demanded protection by the Americans. In exchange he provided Posey with a range of intelligence, including that he had helped Göring steal trainloads of art, that vast stores of treasure had been sent to the Altaussee salt mine and that SS guards had been ordered to blow them all up if they failed to prevent them from falling into Allied hands.

The first part of Bunjes' intelligence corroborated

Bernard O'Connor

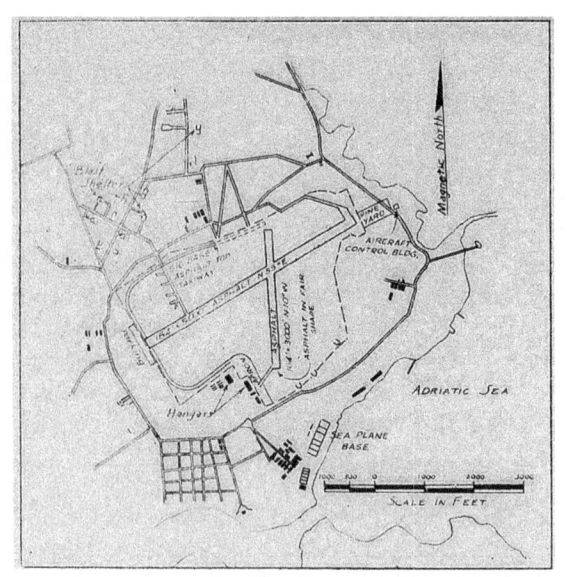

Plan of Brindisi Airfield from where Austrian Bonzos were flown out from in 1944-45. (http://www.forgottenairfields.com/uploads/airfields/italy/apulia/brindisi/brindisi_idroscalo/brindisi-idroscalo-chart-1943.jpg)

Undated aerial photograph of Brindisi Airfield from where the EBENSBURG team was flown to Austria on 8 April 1945. (https://forum.paradoxplaza.com/forum/index.php?threads/visualizing-the-second-world-war.932086/page-9)

Operation EBENSBURG

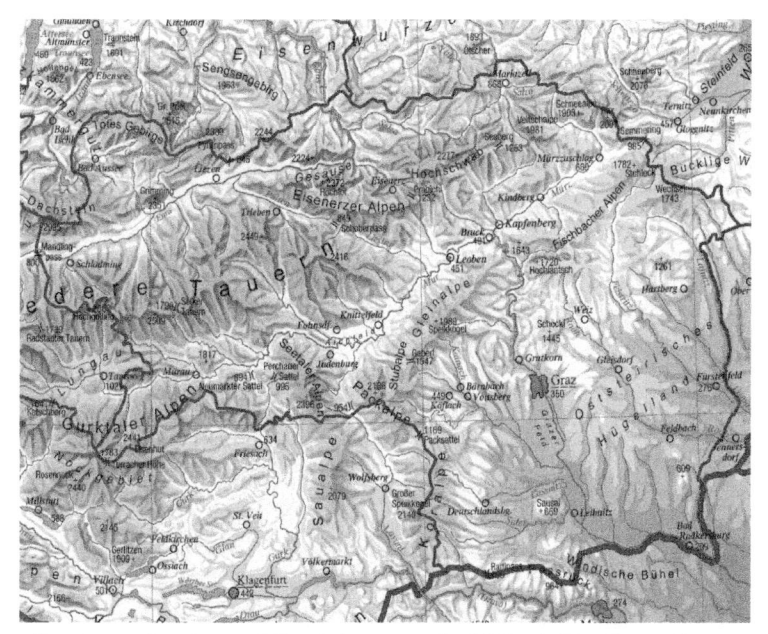

Panoramic view of Bad Aussee (middle left), Grundlsee and Töplitzee. (https://static2.bergfex.com/images/downsized/79/ f8e096f8ad7ea679_4d7b7a94a89a6208.jpg)

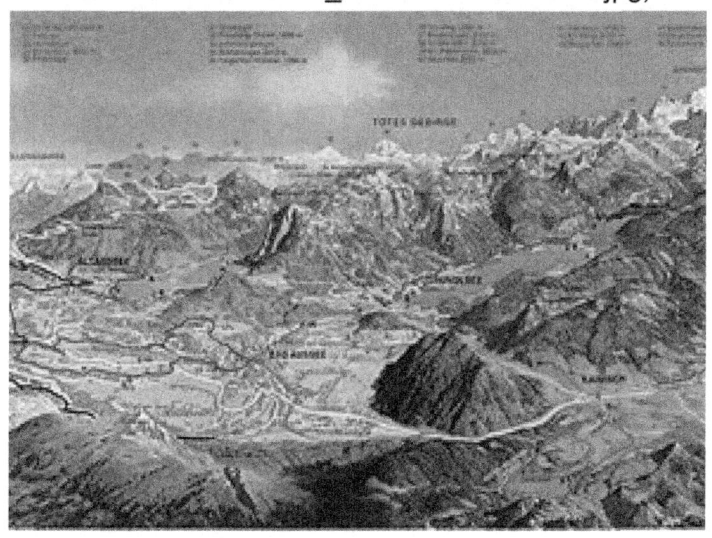

Relief map of Styria showing Bad Aussee in the northwest corner. (http://www.gifex.com/fullsize-en/2011-07-04-14031/ Physical-map-of-Styria.html)

Bernard O'Connor

Sepp Plieseis, Austrian resistance leader in the Bad Aussee area.
(http://ooe.kpoe.at/article.php/20150225134129974)

Alois Raudaschl who helped remove the bombs from Altaussee mine in May 1945. (Clip from 'Hitlers Schatz im Berg')

Operation EBENSBURG

1945 photograph of the Altaussee salt mine (www.aaa.si.edu)

Undated photograph of the Altaussee Salt works where much of the Nazis' looted art was stored. (http://www.historiassegundaguerramundial.com/lugares/las-minas-de-sal-de-altaussee/?lang=en#prettyPhoto[979982]/0/)

Bernard O'Connor

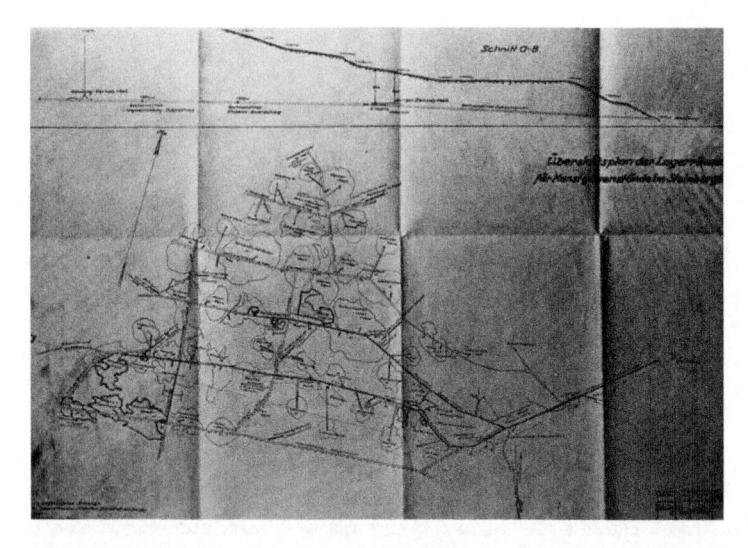

Plan of Alt Aussee salt mine from Robert Posey's notebooks
(https://www.monumentsmenfoundation.org/archives/
documents)

Villa Castiglione, Grundlsee, headquarters of Oberstgruppenführer Ernst Kaltenbrunner in early 1945 and where Hitler's Linz library books were stored. (https://upload.wikimedia.org/wikipedia/commons/thumb/1/14/ Villa_Castiglioni_Grundlsee.jpg/1024px-Villa_Castiglioni_Grundlsee.jpg)

Ernst Kaltenbrunner, the Austrian Chief of the Reichsicherheithauptamt (Reich Central Security Office) (https://prabook.com/web/ernst.kaltenbrunner/1344968)

Kerry Villa, Altaussee, where Kaltenbrunner had a wireless station. (http://azdak.livejournal.com/170003.html)

Gaiswinkler's testimony but whether Posey had been informed about his knowledge beforehand is unknown. (Nicholas, Lynn, *The Rape of Europa: The Fate of Europe's Treasures in the Third Reich and the Second World War*, Vintage, 1995, p.332; Charney, op.cit. pp.238-40)

It is possible that Bunjes informed Posey that, with the advance of Allied forces on Berlin, Hitler had ordered the 'Nero Decree'.

In February 1945, a telegram from the British Embassy in Bern to the Ministry of Economic Warfare in London reported that an important part of the Berlin State Collections was stored in flak towers at the Berlin Zoo and in Friedrichshain. It also stated that salt mines at Ischl and Alt Aussee in Austria were the largest art depositories, containing the Linz museum collection, the Rosenberg collection and Austrian state collections. Schloss Nikolsburg, northeast of Vienna on the Czech border, was the property of Fürst Dietrichstein and an important depository of looted art. The Liechtenstein state collections were partly stored in Schloss Gamming at Mariazell and in Stift Kloster at Neuburg, both in Austria. (TNA FO 837/1154/3)

Having helped liberate France, US General Patton's Third Army moved into the Rhineland where Posey informed Patton and the US tactical commanders about the Altaussee salt mine. In April 1945, as SHAEF had determined the Russians would reach Berlin before the Allies and that they had intelligence that the Nazis were planning a last-ditch stand in the Alpenfortress, they redirected the Third Army to Czechoslovakia and Austria. Accompanying it were two Monuments Men, Captain Robert K. Posey and Private Lincoln Kirstein. Whether they were aware that the Red Army had a 'Trophy Brigade' which acquired Nazi-looted works of arts as restitution for the loss of an estimated 20 million people during their conflict with Germany is unknown. If so, not only did the Monuments Men want to prevent the destruction of the Altaussee mine, they also wanted to get there before the Russians. According to Jim Morrison of the Smithsonian Museum, 'it's estimated they [the Trophy Brigade] stole millions of objects, including Old Master drawings, paintings and books.' (Morrison, op.cit.)

Although artworks were not mentioned in Hitler's decree, their resale value to the Russians or the Allies was thought to have been enormous. Charney disputed that the artworks' destruction was Hitler's intention as his will specified his desire that the Linz collection be given to the state and installed in the proposed Führermuseum.

According to Grafl, in early April, Martin Bormann, the Nazi Party Secretary and Hitler's private secretary, wrote to Gauleiter August Eigruber, the Nazi leader in control of Upper Austria, instructing him to destroy the Altaussee salt mine with all its contents. (Harclerode and Pittaway, p. 101, from their interview with Josef Grafl, 13 July 1998)

On 13 April, Dr Helmut von Hummel, Bormann's secretary, Gauinspektor Glinz and other officials arrived at Altaussee with instructions to seal the mine's entrance. Von Hummel informed Pöchmüller that Albert Speer, the Nazi Minister of Armaments and Hitler's confidant, had persuaded the Führer not to include non-industrial sites in the destruction order but to incapacitate them so as to be of no immediate value to the Allies. Two bombs were put in place and detonators provided to explode them. Von Hummel then left with a crate reported to have contained about 2,000 gold coins. (TNA FO 1020/2766/1; Harclerode and Pittaway, op.cit. p.109)

According to Pöchmüller,'s testimony, he went to Linz to inform Eigruber about von Hummel's visit but was told that confirmation of this new order was needed from Hitler himself. 'The main point is total destruction. On this point, we will remain bull-headed.' If he had to, he would 'personally come and throw grenades into the mine.' (Charney, op.cit. p.253-4) On 13 April, Eigruber was reported to have said that he did not want to let the art treasures fall into the hands of the Bolsheviks, and 'under no circumstances fall into the hands of the world Jewry.' (https://www.profil.at/home/der-salzberg-altaussee-hollywood-thriller-351944)

Charney reported how Pöchmüller was dismayed by Eigruber's reaction but, with the agreement of Otto Högler, the mine's foreman, and Eberhard Mayerhoffer, the technical director, they planned to lay 'palsy charges', charges which would explode to paralyse operations by blocking the entrance to the mine while preserving its contents. Eigruber was convinced the explosives would cause the mine to collapse onto the artworks, but to make sure, he ordered more bombs. According to one source, eight crates weighing 1,100 pound [about 500kg] were delivered sometime in April.

(Morrison, Jim, *The True Story of the Monuments Men*, Smithsonian.com) A further four were reported to have been delivered on 30 April. (https://www.profil.at/home/der-salzberg-altaussee-hollywood-thriller-351944)Ibid.)

    A young boy brought Gaiswinkler a message from the miners that a mysterious convoy heavily guarded by SS men had arrived at the mine. It consisted of six large wooden crates marked MARMOR NICHT STÜRZEN (Marble do not drop). Supervised by the local Nazi leader and his immediate superior, the regional inspector for the Upper Region, Herr Glinz, they had to load the crates on to the mine trolleys, a job that required a number of men as they were very heavy. What puzzled the men was that the explosives expert and director of mines, Herr Kain, was also present and that SS men were guarding the entrance to the mine. The loaded trolleys were carefully pushed along a narrow-gauge track to the entrance of the mine shaft. What their contents were was a mystery, even to the mining officials. (de Jaeger, op.cit. p.127-8)

    Gaiswinkler instructed two miners, thought to include Raudaschl, to find out what was in the crates. During a night shift, they avoided the guards by using passages they knew, located one of the crates, forced it open and discovered underneath straw covering a 500-pound (227kg) unexploded US-made aerial bomb. There was no detonator attached. They reported their discovery to Gaiswinkler and Professor Michel, who now realised the sinister intentions of the SS. Six such bombs were more than enough to blow up the entire mine and its contents. (Charney, op.cit. p.254)

    The following night, without the knowledge of the SS guards, Michel, assisted by the female photographer working with him and two miners, transferred the most important works to the chapel dedicated to St Barbara, the patron saint of miners, which was thought to be safe from any explosions. On 28 April, Pöchmüller ordered Högler to 'remove all eight crates of marble recently stored within the mines in agreement with Bergungsbeauftragter Dr Seiber and to deposit these in a shed which to you appears suitable as a temporary storage depot. You are further instructed to prepare the palsy charge as soon as possible. The point in time when the palsy is supposed to take place will only be presented to you by myself personally.'

Although Glinz overheard the arrangements to move the crates and ordered six SS guards to be stationed at the entrance to the mine 24 hours a day, he was not aware of Pöchmüller's role, nor of the plastic charges. (Charney, op.cit. pp.255-6)

Gaiswinkler and Pöchmüller's post-war accounts failed to acknowledge each other's assistance, but it is thought that they must have collaborated. Gaiswinkler's group was not powerful enough to take over the mine from the Germans, and when he learnt that Austrian SS-Obersturmbannführer Otto Skorzeny and 800 SS troops were advancing towards the Bad Aussee area, there were worries about what reprisals would be taken against the local population. A propaganda campaign was introduced. He ordered the take-over of Vienna II, the powerful relay transmitter at Teichschloss in Bad Aussee, and broadcast fake news. The much-feared partisans supporting Yugoslav General Tito were reported to be advancing out of Slovenia and planning a large-scale parachute drop in the area. To give the Germans the impression that some had already arrived, he ordered lots of fires to be lit in the mountains to indicate troops had set up camp and were signalling. (de Jaeger, op.cit. p.128-9)

Grafl reported that 'It was an alarmingly easy operation. We put an Austrian on the air who said repeatedly "This is Austria, red, white and red." There was no resistance to it at all. We didn't have many resources with which to defend the transmitter. If the Germans had wanted to, they could have taken it back quite easily. But they did nothing.' (Quoted in Harclerode and Pittaway, op.cit. p.111)

They also broadcast misleading reports to confuse the enemy forces, forcing them to drive on routes where the Resistance were lying in wait to ambush them. In this way, Grafl reported, 'We were able to take weapons and vehicles from SS officers without any trouble at all.' (Ibid.) Wilkinson reported them obtaining tanks from the Germans, but other reports mention armoured cars.

They infiltrated German Army and SS formations disguised as officers where they spread alarm and confusion by issuing as many conflicting orders as they could think of. This strategy proved particularly effective in hampering the Nazi's efforts to defend the whole Ausseerland as part of the "Inner Fortress". TNA HS7/146 German directorate history

Part I (continued): Austria, Sudetenland)

Fearing hardened opposition from Tito's partisans, from the Russians who had reached Linz and from the Americans who had reached Salzburg, Skorzeny gave the order to retreat.

Using two captured armoured personnel carriers, Resistance members wearing captured SS uniforms were able to kidnap Franz Blaha, Eigruber's deputy, and two leaders of the local Gestapo unit. Blaha reported that he had been given responsibility for the destruction of the mine but as the Nazis' lines of communication between Austria and Germany had been cut, there was chaos with local officers uncertain about giving commands without orders from their superiors. Neither Bormann nor von Hummel could be contacted. (Charney, op.cit. p.256)

At the mine, time was running out, and the miners decided to take action themselves. They knew that the detonators for the bombs were also stored at the mine. They suggested to Professor Michel that they blast all but the main entrance to the mine with small charges that would block free passage to, but not damage the interior, and, desperate as he was, Michel agreed to their suggestion. Gaiswinkler meanwhile had heard from his agents that orders had come from Eigruber and Kaltenbrunner to blow up the mine, and that a special demolition squad of reliable SS men had already been detailed to carry out this task. He decided on immediate action. He telephoned Kaltenbrunner and told him the order must be countermanded. When Kaltenbrunner refused, one of his aides – now in the Resistance – persuaded him to change his mind. Kaltenbrunner countermanded the order. (de Jaeger, op.cit. pp.130-31)

Charney credited Alois Raudaschl with the approach to Kaltenbrunner. Having a mutual friend who lived near Villa Castiglione, a meeting was arranged at which Kaltenbrunner's 'sense of nationalism and desire to preserve the irreplaceable cultural icons' persuaded him to countermand Eigruber's order. (Charney, op.cit. pp. 257-8)

With Kaltenbrunner's permission to remove the bombs, a team of miners set to work. Michel claimed later that he had been responsible for the removal of the mines. According to Charney,

The miners spent four hours removing the bombs and their crates. At midnight, as the bomb removal was nearly complete, another of Eigruber's henchmen, Tank Staff Sergeant Haider, arrived at the mine. Seeing what was afoot, he threatened that, if the bombs were removed, Eigruber himself would "come himself to Alt Aussee ...and hang each and every one of you himself."
Fearful of repercussions, Raudaschl contacted Kaltenbrunner, who personally phoned Eigruber at 1.30 am on 4 May, hours after Sergeant Haider's threat, ordering Eigruber to allow the bomb removal. Eigruber relented and said that no repercussions would be taken. The SS guards were instructed by Eigruber to allow the miners into the mine, and Haider could only watch. (Charney, op.cit. p.258)

However, annoyed at what he believed was Kaltenbrunner's betrayal, Eigruber ordered a demolition squad of SS men from Innsbruck equipped with flamethrowers and explosives to destroy the mine and the Linz Library Collection at Villa Castiglione. When Gaiswinkler's informers at Kaltenbrunner's headquarters informed him, he ordered an armed defence of the mine and Villa Castiglione. A last-minute struggle by armed Resistance fighters saved the villa from destruction, but the mine's safety was uncertain. Fearing the imminent arrival of the Americans, the SS guards at the mine fled up into the mountains to join other SS troops. (de Jaeger, op.cit. pp.130-31; Harclerode and Pittaway, op.cit. p.111)

According to a 1995 Kammerhof Museum publication about Gaiswinkler's role in Bad Aussee during the war, 'On 3 May, the combined force of his team, the miners and members of the Resistance established a defensive perimeter and secured the area of the mine. The miners, whose principal motivation was the preservation of the mine and their livelihood, suggested to Michel and Gaiswinkler that the six bombs and their detonators should be removed and the main tunnel of the mine demolished with explosives, sealing it off. Both agreed, and the miners set to work removing the bombs. Two days later on 5 May, the main tunnel was blown up, leaving the repository and its priceless contents sealed safely inside.' ('Die Rettung der Kuntzschütze im Altausee Bergwerk', Bad Aussee, 1995; Quoted in Harclerode and Pittaway, op.cit. p.111-112)

Charney reported that at dawn on 5 May, preparation for the destruction of the mine's entrance began. Gaiswinkler, Standhartinger and Lzicar had all received sabotage training in England, but there was no mention of them giving advice to the miners. While the mine probably had its own explosives experts and the wherewithal to undertake the destruction, it seems quite possible that SOE had parachuted 'sweets and toys', their euphemism for sabotage equipment.

'As soon as the charges were ready, the miners who had spent the past two weeks laying the palsy charge threw the detonator switch. Six tons of explosives linked to 502 timing switches and 386 detonators sealed 137 tunnels in the Alt Aussee salt mine, the world's greatest museum of stolen art. There was nothing Eigruber could do to harm what lay locked inside.' (Charney, op.cit. pp.258-9)

Scouts belonging to General Fabianku's Sixth Army were reported to have heard the explosions and seen that the SS guards had left. When Fabianku was informed, on 6 May he ordered an attack on the Resistance's headquarters. Against well-armed and motivated men, the attack failed.

Eigruber's destruction order also included the demolition of the German's research station on the banks of Töplitzee. The explosions Gaiswinkler had been told about while he was in the Luftwaffe could have been blowing up the hillside to make the road to the site but also from in the lake itself. When he was back in Bad Aussee, more explosions were heard, so Standhartinger and Lzicar were sent to reconnoitre the area. They reported that it had been used by the Kriegsmarine, Germany's navy, for the development of sonic mines and torpedoes but that it had been destroyed. Eigruber would not have wanted the Allies to benefit from the German research and technology. (de Jaeger p.130-1; Harclerode and Pittaway, op.cit. p. 112; Charney, op.cit. pp.256-7)

Locals also reported seeing the Germans dumping boxes into the lake. In a conversation after the war with de Jaeger, Hoettl told him that,

A few years after the war, [...] fishermen on the lake noticed a steady stream of banknotes floating on the surface. On closer inspection, these proved to be five-, ten- and twenty-pound sterling notes. The police were alerted; bank officials were called in. the notes, after careful checking, proved to be fakes. Hoettl found himself confronted by his former wartime activities and was able to throw more light on the story.

It was Heydrich who had proposed to Hitler that they flood non-belligerent countries with faked English money in order to ruin the British economy abroad. Hitler had endorsed the idea and Hoettl, among others, had been involved in its execution. The most accomplished forgers, many of them in German gaols and concentration camps, were rounded up and eventually placed under strict guard in a camp near Ebensee. They were well looked after and given every possible facility for their work. In his fascinating book *Hitler's Paper War* (1955), Hoettl has described how the forgers were able to produce almost faultless notes which only the Bank of England could detect as fakes. When the American forces were advancing on the area, it became imperative to hide the printing-plates and all the evidence – and the nearest lake that was considered deep enough was Lake Töplitz. Over the years the wooden boxes became waterlogged and the notes inside swelled and burst the boxes. (de Jaeger, op.cit. pp.135-6)

The arrival of the Americans and the rescue of the stolen artworks

There are conflicting accounts of the arrival of the American forces at the mine. According to the EBENSBURG team's personnel files, they arrived in Austria four days before the Americans. This appears to be an error and four weeks would be more accurate. During the fighting against Fabianku's troops, Gaiswinkler sent two scouts, Leopold Köberl and Julius Stockl, to the Pötschen Pass to meet the vanguard of the Third Army and ask for their help. He had received reports that they were in Vöcklabruck, about 50km northeast of Salzburg. The Americans wanted intelligence from the resistance about access to the mine and what defences might be expected.

On their return trip, Köberl and Stockl were stopped at an SS roadblock and arrested. When this was discovered, a rescue mission by other Resistance members was mounted which saved them from certain execution.

On 7 May, the German forces signed an unconditional surrender at Reims. Gaiswinkler and some of his men drove their two armoured personnel carriers with the red, white and red Austrian flag flying, to meet the Americans. By that time, most of the estimated 6,000 German troops which had been in the area were in retreat. There was a great sense of relief when the US 80th Infantry Division under the command of Major Ralph Pearson arrived at the mine the following day, 8th May. Met by Michel, who was one of only a few in the area who spoke English, they were given his account of how the mine and its contents were saved.

Gaiswinkler was not at the mine to meet the Americans. He had heard that one of his couriers had been arrested and sent to Bad Mittendorf to be shot. According to his testimony, in retaliation, he and his team launched a surprise counterattack on Fabianku's headquarters. Having crept through the snow-covered pine forest, they caught the camp off-guard, kidnapped the General and took him to their headquarters. Faced with being shot himself unless he ordered the courier's release, he agreed.

As the mine's entrance tunnel was blocked, the miners were unsure how much rubble there was to clear away. They estimated it could take up to a fortnight but when they got to work, they cleared enough to allow Posey and Kirstein access. They spent four days examining and cataloguing the artworks, valued at that time to be $500,000. (Ibid.p.131; Harclerode and Pittaway, op.cit. p.112-3; Charney, op.cit. p.264)

Using Thomas Howe's *Saltmines and Castles* and an OSS report on the collections, Harclerode and Pittaway detailed the contents of the mine.

As they worked their way into the mine, Posey and Kirstein discovered a number of huge caverns and galleries interconnected by a honeycomb of tunnels. One of these caverns was known as the Springerwerke. Measuring about 50 feet in length and 30 feet in width, it contained about 2,000 paintings stored in two tiers of racking around the three sides of the cavern and down the centre. Among the items discovered in this cavern examined by Posey and Kirstein were around forty Italian paintings of the famous Linz collection from Amsterdam, along with paintings by Brueghel, Titian, Rembrandt, Tintoretto, van Dyck, Rubens, Reynolds, Nattier, Lancret and Hals.

The largest of the caverns was the Kammergraf, which lay three-quarters of a mile from the entrance of the mine. This comprised several galleries which were on different levels and were so high that those on the first level could accommodate three tiers of paintings on racks. Among the numerous paintings secreted here were works by Titian, Tintoretto, van Dyck, Rubens, Rembrandt and Veronese. Many of them had been appropriated from private owners in Austria, the Netherlands, Belgium and France, including the Rothschild Gutmann and Mannheimer collections. Others were from the Dutch Goudstikker and French Sammlung Berta collections. Also found in the Kammergraf, which was devoted for works from the Linz collections, was the fourteenth-century Hohenfurth altarpiece; drawings and paintings from the sixteenth to the eighteenth centuries; tapestries from Krakow Castle in Poland; cases of porcelain; decorations from the Reichkanslei in Berlin; and furniture from the castle at Posen. The most important discovery in the Kammergraf, however, was Vermeer's *Portrait of the Artist in His Studio*. Other major works stacked nearby in the Kammergraf were some of the fifteen paintings and sculptures removed from the famous monastery at Monte Cassino in Italy. These included Raphael's *Madonna of the Divine Love,* Titian's *Danae*, an *Annunciation Annunciation* by Filippino Lippi, *Crucifixion* by van Dyck, *Sacra Conversazione* by Palma Vecchio, Sebastiano de Piombo's *Portrait of Pope Clement VI,* Peter Brueghel's *The Blind leading the Blind,* and a landscape by Claude Lorrain.

However, it was on entering the mine's chapel, - a cavern called the Kapelle and complete with an altar carved in salt – that Posey made the most important discovery. There to his great joy was the Ghent altarpiece, van Dyck's *Adoration of the Mystic Lamb;* the principal item he had been seeking, which [...] Hermann Bunjes had assured him was at Alt Aussee. Shortly afterwards it was moved to a more secure location in another cavern, the Mineral

Kabinett, where it was placed under lock and key. The altarpiece was one of the two most important single items in the mine, the other being Michelangelo's statue *The Madonna of Bruges,* which Posey and Kirstein subsequently found in the Kaiser Josef cavern. The Kapelle cavern also contained Archduke Franz Ferdinand's collection of Spanish arms and armour, which belonged to Czechoslovakia, and the Linz coin collection.

As they made their way further into the mine, Posey and Kirstein discovered a large of paintings in another cavern called the Mondberg; among these were several sixteenth-century Venitian works including Paris Bordone's *Portrait of a Young Woman.* Subsequent reports stated the mine contained in total some 6,775 paintings, principally Old Masters, which had been intended for the Führermuseum. Other items included a large number of nineteenth-century German paintings, over 2,000 drawings and watercolours, in excess of 900 prints, some 130 pieces of sculpture, collections of books and manuscripts, (including those of the Biblioteca Herziana in Rome), archives, tapestries, collections of coins and armour, and the Millionen Zimmer and Chinesiches Kabinett from the Imperial Summer Palace at Schönbrunn. One particularly interesting item found by Captain Posey was a letter from Martin Bormann, directing that at all costs, the repository should not be permitted to be captured by Allied forces but that its contents must not be harmed. (Harclerode and Pittaway, p.114-5; Howe, Thomas, *Salt Mines and Castles,* Bobbs Merrill, New York, 1946, pp.147-53; OSS ALIU CIR No. 4, Scope of the Collections, pp.78-9)

Apart from the legitimately stored works of art from the Vienna Museum, also found in the salt mine were the imperial crown and regalia of the Austrian Empire. In another mine they found strongboxes containing 4½ million Reichsmarks of army funds. Hidden in the garden of Kerry Villa they unearthed 50kg of gold bars, fifty cases of other gold, $2 million, $2 million in Swiss francs, 5 cases of jewels, a stamp collection worth 5 million gold marks. 80,000kg of sugar, 75,000 tins of sardines and canned meat, quantities of tobacco and cigarettes and military documents. (de Jaeger, op.cit. p.132; http://conspiracy-cafe.blogspot.co.uk/2016/12/nazi-trivia-villa-kerry-altaussee.html)

The Art Looting Investigation Unit of the OSS produced a Consolidated Interrogation Report on Hitler's Museum and Library in Linz. Chapter VII provided a summary of the scope of the collection, amassed mainly at the Alt Aussee salt mine in Austria, under the title 'Fuehrervorbehalt'.

The May 1945 inventory of material destined for Linz included a total of 5,350 paintings by old masters, 21 contemporary German paintings, 230 drawings and watercolours, 1,039 prints, 95 tapestries, 68 sculptures, 32 cases of coins, 128 items of arms and armours, 64 items of furniture, 79 baskets and 43 cases of objets d'art, 237 cases of books for the Linz library sent from Grundlsee and the Gordon Craig theatre archive, presumably destined for the Linz theatre. The Alt Aussee inventory also included a number of works of art 'which may or may not have been destined for Linz', including 209 paintings and rugs for the Fuehrer's private castle in Posen, 534 paintings, 9 tapestries, 16 sculptures, 11 rugs, 7 portfolios of prints and 16 cases of objets d'art for Hitler's house at Berchtesgaden, 119 cases of books from Hitler's private library in Berlin, the Ghent and Louvain altarpieces, Michelangelo's Madonna, 11 paintings from Bruges and 17 paintings and 11 cases of sculptures and bronzes from Monte Cassino. It also lists the contents of ten smaller depositories of Linz material and includes a table indicating the dates and quantities of works of art shipped from Munich to Alt Aussee, Kremsmunster and Hohenfurth. (TNA T 209/29/15, Folder 3. Supplement dated 15 January 1946 to the Consolidated Interrogation Report No 4 by the Art Looting Investigation Unit of the OSS on Hitler's Museum and Library in Linz)

Major Edward 'Teddy' Croft-Murray who had been the Assistant Keeper of Prints and Drawings at the British Museum before the war, was one of the Monuments Men sent to Alt Aussee. He had been attached to the MFAA in Italy in 1943 with Lieutenant Frederick Hartt and Captains Deane Keller, Roderick Enthoven and Roger Ellis. In mid-May 1944, they were told that treasures reported missing from the Abbey at Monte Cassino had been found at Alt Aussee salt mine.

In early July 1944 he was inspecting the treasures found in the Palazzo Reale in Caserta which had been the Italian Aviation College and a German headquarters. When the mine at Alt Aussee was secured, he was sent with Lieutenant Colonel Humphrey Brooke, fellow Monuments Man, to document the contents. They arrived on 23 July to find Lieutenant Commander George Stout busy organising the packing and shipment. He had been there since 21 May. (https://www.monumentsmenfoundation.org/the-heroes/the-monuments-men/croft-murray-maj.-edward)

A small gauge railway was installed to allow the contents to be removed from the mine where they were loaded onto trucks and taken under armed guard to the Munich Collection Point, Hitler's former headquarters.

To prevent the artwork falling into Russian hands, Stout was ordered to empty and transport the mine's contents by 1 July. According to Morrison,

> It was an impossible order. "Loaded less than two trucks by 11.30," Stout wrote on June 18. "Too slow. Need larger crew."
>
> By June 24, Stout extended the workdaly to 4 a.m. to 10 p.m., but the logistics were daunting. Communication was difficult; he was often unable to contact Posey. There weren't enough trucks for the trip to the collecting point, the former Nazi headquarters in Munich, 150 miles away. There wasn't enough packing material. Finding food and billets for the men proved difficult. And it rained. "All hands grumbling," Stout wrote.
>
> By July 1, the boundaries [between US and Red Army troops] had not been settled so Stout and his crew moved forward. He spent a few days packing the Bruges Madonna, which Nicholas describes as "looking very much like a large Smithfield ham." On July 10, it was lifted onto a mine cart and Stout walked it to the entrance, where it and the Ghent altarpiece were loaded onto trucks. The next morning Stout accompanied them to the Munich collecting point
>
> On July 19, he reported that 80 truckloads, 1,850 paintings, 1,441 cases of paintings and sculpture, 11 sculptures, 30 pieces of furniture and 34 large packages of textiles had been removed from the mine. There was more, but not for Stout who left on the RMS *Queen Elizabeth* on August 6. (Morrison, op.cit.)

American art historian Craig Hugh-Smyth led a team of

scholars in Munich in identifying the owners of the artwork and returning them to each country but there are still items today that remain unclaimed. (Charney, op.cit. p.270)

Although not catalogued, there was evidence that Leonardo da Vinci's masterpiece was amongst the artwork saved. Wilkinson mentioned it is his post-war Government Source Inspection report on British troops in Austria.

RESISTANCE IN BAD AUSSEE

The part played by local resistance groups in hastening the end of Nazi rule in AUSTRIA is well-illustrated in a report on the activities of the underground movement in BAD AUSSEE district during April and early May 1945, which was recently submitted by the Burgomeister of BAD AUSSEE to the Landeshauptmann of Upper Austria. [TNA FO 1020/1252, Gaiswinkler's Aussee Party, Sheet 20, paras, 78-80] The report is clearly that of an interested party, but from what we know of the general context of the facts given, there is no reason to suppose that the picture they present is over-drawn.

In a brief survey of the history of the BAD AUSSEE Resistance Movement to the German collapse last spring, the report states that some 20 assorted Resistance Groups – Communist, Socialist, Christian Social, Monarchist – has for some time been working along more or less independent lines. From time to time, the Nazi authorities struck at the Movements, which suffered many arrests and lost two members killed. The head of the Resistance for the BAD AUSSEE district and GRAZ was one Albrecht GAISWINKLER, who, after an adventurous year of conscripted service in the German army (1943-44), deserted in 1944 after the Allied landings in NORMANDY, and went over to the French Maquis, complete with four car-loads of German arms and ammunition and 500,000 francs from the Battalion's imprest account. GAISWINKLER stayed with the Maquis till 5 September 1944, when he managed to make his way through to the American lines, bringing with him, as prisoners, 17 German soldiers. The Allies decided that they could make good use of him, and on the night of 8/9 April 1945 GAISWINKLER was accordingly parachuted down into the Salzkammergut to resume his activities with the Austrian resistance. This he did to such good effect that within 3 weeks he had collected together a well-armed and well-organised band of 360 men.

The report then goes on to describe the part played by GAISWINKLER and his men during the confused days of early May 1945, after the Nazi regime had collapsed or had reached the point of collapse, and before the Allied troops had moved in to take over in its place. During this period the BAD AUSSEE Resistance groups seized and imprisoned all the leading Gestapo, SD and Party officials in the district and took over control of the local Gendarmerie. They managed to prevent the destruction, planned by the Nazis, of the ALT AUSSEE salt works, whose mines were used by the Germans as a storehouse for looted art treasures, and in this way saved such precious objects as the Louvre Mona Lisa, the Austrian Imperial Crown, and other treasures to the value of many millions of pounds.

The Resistance Movement was also able to hasten the end of that part of the German Sixth Army which found itself, in early May, in the BAD AUSSEE Area. According to the report, their most successful technique here, apart from the usual tactics of attacking convoys and railways, was to infiltrate into Army and SS formations disguised as officers, and there to spread alarm and confusion by issuing as many conflicting orders as they could think of. This technique proved especially effective in hampering the efforts of the Germans to defend the whole AUSSEERLAND as part of the "Inner Fortress". From the German Sixth Army, the partisans also secured some tanks, and thus became the only Austrian Regiment to possess any armour.

Equally valuable though less spectacular work was done by the BAD AUSSEE partisans in seizing prominent Nazis and other arrestable persons (who might have escaped in the confusion of the general collapse) and in taking steps themselves to replace all undesirable local civil servants, police officials, etc., so that, when the Allies did arrive, it was a more or less ordered community which they came to take over.

In all these activities, the BAD AUSSEE partisans consider themselves so successful that when the Americans marched in, the words of the report "not a single house, bridge or street in AUSSEERLAND was blown up and not a single shot was fired", and, as regards de-Nazification measures, "there was not a single Buergermeister, or police official left who was not, and who had not always been, a true Austrian." (TNA HS7/146 German directorate history Part I (continued): Austria, Sudetenland)

Wilkinson's 1945 report on the History of the Clowder Mission acknowledged Gaiswinkler's role.

Two weeks before the Americans arrived, GAISWINKLER was in virtual command of the district. He was able to hand over to the occupying troops a smoothly functioning administration, completely purged of all Nazi elements. His assistance was instrumental in securing the arrest of KALTENBRUNNER and his associates, the preservation of the MONA LISA, the Austrian Crown Jewels, and several million marks worth of foreign currency and specie which had been concealed in the salt mines. Many of the leading Nazis and the Commander of the 6th Army were already in his hands. Nowhere in Austria can Military Government have been presented with an easier task. In recognition of this GAISWINKLER was immediately appointed BEZIRKSHAUPTMANN by the Americans. (Imperial War Museum, 03 56/11/2/2 History of Clowder Mission. Wilkinson Papers; TNA WO 204/10249)

Harclerode and Pittaway's investigations revealed that an Austrian Government Gendarmerie Command report, dated 12 December 1945, stated that the *Mona Lisa* from Paris had been among the 80 wagons of art and cultural objects from across Europe that had been packed into the salt mine. Another report stated that some crates were sent straight to the Louvre in Paris instead of to Munich, arriving on 17 June 1945. They determined that although the Louvre staff removed the painting for safe-keeping at the start of the war, a nearly identical 16th copy was packed in a wooden crate labelled *Mona Lisa*. It was this copy the Germans had taken to Altausse and which is now reported hanging outside the museum director's office. This was confirmed in Professor William Mackenzie's official history of the SOE in which he described Gaiswinkler as 'the star turn of the Austrian Resistance'. (Harclerode and Pittaway, op.cit. pp.116-20;

Charney, op.cit. p.268; Evans, Michael (2001). 'Mona Lisa 'was saved from Nazis by British agent', http://www.thetimes.co.uk/article/0,,47575,00.html; Mackenzie, William, *The Secret History of S.O.E.: Special Operations Executive, 1940-1945*, St Ermin's Press, 2002, p.453)

Gaiswinkler's help in the Americans' arrest of leading Nazi officials

Robert Matteson, the Chief of the 80th Infantry Division's Counter Intelligence Corps reported in 'The Last Days of Ernst Kaltenbrunner' that, assisted by Sydney Bruskin, the 319th Regiment interpreter, they had received intelligence from one of the leaders of the Austrian Freedom Movement that top SS officials were still in the area. 80% of the arrests of SS, Gestapo, Sicherheitdienst and Austrian Nazi Party leaders he attributed to this intelligence.

Thanks to Gaiswinkler's effective groundwork, Sid and I were able to arrest this group, seal its headquarters at the Kerry Villa, and stop the operation of its transmitter. We did not know then that this was the central communications center for the National Redoubt and Kaltenbrunner's only connection with the outside world; its importance and the feverish activities of the Goettsch-Waneck group during the preceding month were revealed only later after detailed interrogation of the principals. For the moment our attention was all on locating Kaltenbrunner, and these people gave no leads on his whereabouts except the information that he had been at Alt Aussee on May 3.

... We located and arrested many lesser Nazis who had fled to Alt Aussee, seeking, for the most part, to collect their thoughts and prepare their anti-Nazi alibis – Gunther Altenburg, Minister Plenipotentiary to Greece; General Erich Alt of the Luftwaffe; Joseph Heider, who had been detailed by Eigruber to blow up the Alt Aussee salt mines wherein was stored a fabulous collection of looted art treasures for the projected Great Hitler Museum at Linz; Dr Hjalmar Mae, head of the pupper state in Estonia; Walter Riedel, construction chief for the V-2 weapons at Peenemunde; Ernst Szargarus, Foreign Office Secretary in Rome; Spiros The first important contact was with Albrecht Gaiswinkler, a

British agent who had been parachuted into the area on April 20 [sic]. A native of Bad Aussee, he had been drafted into the Wehrmacht, had deserted in France, turning a Nazi supply train over to the French Maquis, and when the Third Army liberated Alsace had given himself up to the Americans. The Americans had turned him over to the British, to whom the Aussee area was allocated for future occupation. Gaiswinkler had learned that Wilhelm Waneck, Chief of the RSHA [Reichssicherheitshauptamt, the Reich's Main Security Office] Intelligence Section for Southeastern Europe - and one of Kaltenbrunner's May 3 conferees at Strobl [A conference between leading SS officers) -was now operating a wireless transmitting station in the Kerry Villa located on a hill at the outskirts of Alt Aussee. Working with Waneck were his deputy, Wilhelm Hoettl, (another of the conferees), Werner Goettsch, who had earlier held Waneck's job and now was a sort of chief ideologist for the RSHA, and a number of other Nazi officials

Hadji Kyriakos, Under Governor of the National Bank of occupied Greece; William Knothe, General Counsel of the Foreign Office; Dr Carlos Wetzell, head of the pharmaceutical industry; and Dr Bailent Homan, a minister in the Hungarian puppet government. (Matteson, Robert, *The Last Days of Ernst Kaltenbrunner,* Studies in Intelligence, CIA Publication, 1960, pp. A17-18)

As the American tank division approached what they thought was the Redoubt, they found the Ebensee concentration camp and Matteson's article details their findings. He went on to describe how they apprehended Kaltenbrunner's wife, mistress and children, from whom they learned of his mountain hideout. Having thrown his uniform into a lake and assuming a disguise as a civilian doctor, he was apprehended with his bodyguards when his mistress called out his name when she saw him marching with a group of prisoners. Interrogated by the Americans and then by the British, despite his help in securing the safety of the Altaussee salt mine and its treasures, he was found guilty of war crimes at the Nuremberg trials and hanged. Eigruber was also captured, convicted or war crimes and hanged. The counsel reported that 'never in the history of the world was so great a collection assembled with so little scruple.' Bunjes committed suicide after killing his family. (Ibid; Charney,

Captain Robert K. Posey, one of the Monuments Men (https://www.monumentsmenfoundation.org/the-heroes/the-monuments-men/posey-capt.-robert-k.

Monuments Men (https://arlesmarten.files.wordpress.com/2014/04/aaaaaaaa.jpg)

Operation EBENSBURG

May 1945 photograph of the Altaussee mine workers, staff and Americans with one of the removed bomb crates. (https://furtherglory.wordpress.com/tag/altaussee-salt-mine/)

Storage racks in Altaussee salt mine https://www.pinterest.com/pin/352054895842973689/

https://commons.wikimedia.org/wiki/
File:Altaussee_Salt_Art_Mine_03.jpg

https://commons.wikimedia.org/wiki/
Category:Altaussee_salt_mine#/media/
File:Altaussee_Salt_Art_Mine_01.jpg)

Operation EBENSBURG

https://commons.wikimedia.org/wiki/
File:Altaussee_Salt_Art_Mine_06.jpg

https://commons.wikimedia.org/wiki/
Category:Altaussee_salt_mine#/media/
File:Altaussee_Salt_Art_Mine_04.jpg

Bernard O'Connor

https://commons.wikimedia.org/wiki/
Category:Altaussee_salt_mine#/media/
File:Altaussee_Salt_Art_Mine_02.jpg

Uncovering part of Van Dyck's Ghent Altarpiece in May 1945. (https://www.tripsavvy.com/altaussee-salt-mines-guide-1507941)

Operation EBENSBURG

Van Dyck's 'Adoration of the Mystic Lamb, part of the Ghent Altarpiece recovered from the Altausee salt mine. (https://www.salzwelten.at/en/altaussee/mine/history/#&gid=1&pid=1)

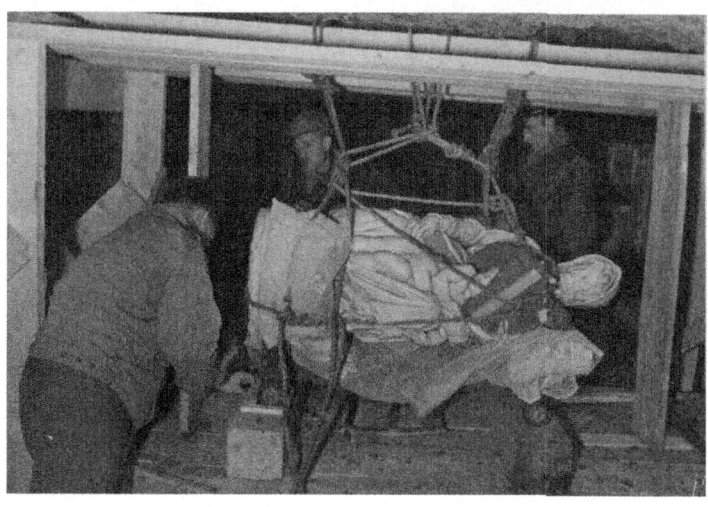

Removing the Madonna from Altaussee salt mine. (https://www.businessinsider.com.au/monuments-men-famous-works-of-art-2014-2

Bernard O'Connor

https://commons.wikimedia.org/wiki/
Category:Altaussee_salt_mine#/media/
File:Lt._Daniel_J._Kern_and_Karl_Sieber_examining_the_Ghent_
Altarpiece_in_the_Altaussee_mine,_1945.jpg

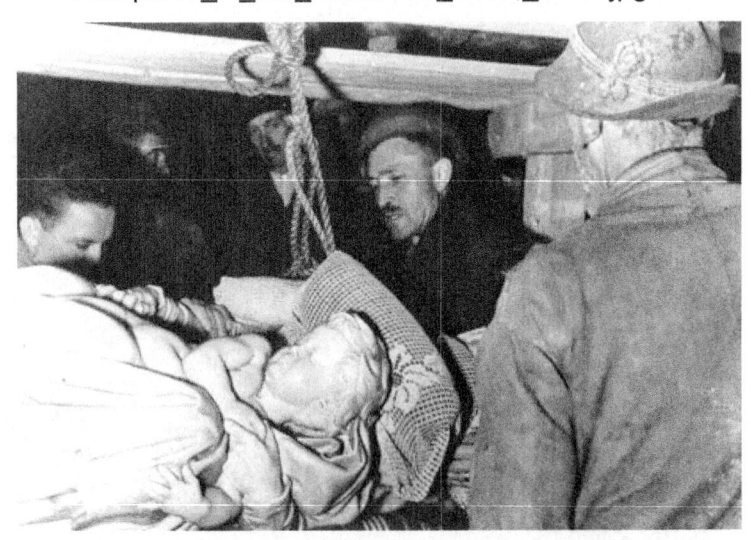

Recovering the statue of Michelangelo's Madonna from Altaussee. (https://en.wikipedia.org/wiki/Nazi_plunder#/media/
File:Bruegger_Madonna_Altaussee.jpg)

Operation EBENSBURG

https://commons.wikimedia.org/wiki/
Category:Altaussee_salt_mine#/media/

Bruegel painting found in Altaussee (https://www.profil.at/home/
der-salzberg-altaussee-hollywood-thriller-351944

Bernard O'Connor

Extract from contemporary document identifying the Mona Lisa as one of the mine's contents. (Clip from 'Hitlers Schatz im Berg')

A copy of the Mona Lisa was found in Altaussee salt mine. https://www.businessinsider.com.au/monuments-men-famous-works-of-art-2014-2

Operation EBENSBURG

Manet's 'In the Conservatory' found in the Altaussee salt mine. (https://www.businessinsider.com.au/monuments-men-famous-works-of-art-2014-2)

http://aroundwestmount.com/2017/02/15/film-screening-victoria-hall-hitlers-mountain-stolen-art/

op.cit. pp.265, 282)

The head of the Counter Intelligence Corps (CIC) operating with the US Third Army, acknowledged Gaiswinkler as helping them arrest the Kaltenbrunner and a number of high-ranking Nazi officers in their Alpine 'Schlupfwinkel', hide-outs. They learned that Kaltenbrunner had succeeded Reinhard Heydrich, 'The Butcher of Prague, who had been assassinated by two SOE-trained agents in 1942. Following the criticism of Wilhelm Canaris's Abwehr, the Reich's military intelligence service, as failing in its espionage and sabotage missions, and the belief that Canaris was behind assassination attempts on Hitler, Kaltenbrunner had the Schutz Staffel (SS), Hitler's 'Protection Squadron, take over its control.

In time, through the interrogation and testimony of Kaltenbrunner and others, it was possible to piece together the story of his recent efforts to salvage something from the German defeat. On April 18 Himmler had named him Commander in Chief of all forces in southern Europe. He had reorganized his intelligence services as a stay-behind underground network, dividing the command between Otto Skorzeny, head of the sabotage units, and Wilhelm Waneck, whose radio station in the Kerry Villa kept in contact not only with Kaltenbrunner and other centres in the Redoubt and in Germany, but also with stay-behind agents in the southern European capitals. (Matteson, op.cit.)

The Allies appointed Plieseis as their security consultant and he went on to work as Communist Party official in his hometown, Bad Ischl. In his wartime memoirs *From the Ebro to Cachstein: The Life Struggle of an Austrian Worker,* he mentioned Gaiswinkler once as the leader of the 'best group' amongst the resistance fighters. He later retracted it, saying that 'We freedom fighters at that time had no connection with the parachutists and they had no idea of the art that lay in the mine shafts. They parachuted in only a few days earlier, and sought shelter for themselves.' (Charney, op.cit. p. 275)

The EBENSBURG team after the German surrender in May 1945

Towards the end of May, SOE's Austrian Section sent the following message to be translated and broadcast by the BBC's Austrian Service. Whether any of the EBENSBURG team listened is unknown, but one imagines that part of their training would have prepared them for post-liberation work.

Austria and her place in the new Europe is engaging the attention and the sympathetic interest of Great Britain. And this in spite of the pre-occupations with vital domestic and international problems facing this country today. For Europe the war may be over but Great Britain is pledged to contribute to the utmost in cooperation with the United States to the downfall of Japan, the last remaining member of the evil and ill-fated Dreier-Pakt. At home, this country is preparing for a vital general election which is to define in the old and tried democratic ways the future direction of British policy.

And yet Great Britain does not overlook the question of the future of Austria. For it is realised that her position in Europe and the healthy development of her democratic independence will be, as it were, a thermometer to which the world can measure the general health of Europe, can see how quickly the patient is recovering from the severe sickness. In the same way the readiness of the Austrians to make a clean and honest break with the past and the ways and means by which such a break is undertaken and the new Austria built up will be watched by Great Britain and all freedom-loving nations with interest, even with sympathy, but, let us be frank, also with some honest suspicion.

For no useful purpose would be served in forgetting that during the long years of Hitler's war Austrians were fighting in the German army against Britain and all her allies. That is why the very first words of Field Marshall Alexander's proclamation which has been posted in all areas under his command states categorically: "The Allied forces enter Austria as victors inasmuch as Austria has waged war as an integral part of Germany against the United Nations."

That is the truth, and we have to face it, although we could wish that it had been otherwise in view of the former feeling of friendship between England and Austria. Great Britain has been fighting for almost six years; during one of them, the most crucial of all, she was the sole defender of the cause of freedom which, as all Austrians can see today, was also their own cause. Britain's stand then has made it possible today for Austria to regain her independence and her freedom.

Yet during these murderous months, many Austrians were helping to fasten the yoke of Hitlerism and German militarism on to Europe. Had Hitler triumphed there would have been no independence, no freedom for Austria and she would have lost forever her right to make the specific Austrian contribution to the culture and wellbeing of the Continent.

We recognise, on the other hand, that there were Austrians of all parties ready to fight against Hitler and Germany and to pay the price for such opposition.

That is why Britain has never given up the hope to find again an Austria willing to lead her own and independent life and to regain that distinguished place in the community of free peoples which was once hers. This hope was shared by the other enemies of Hitler's Third Reich and was expressed in the famous Moscow Declaration which may well be described as the Magna Carta of the new Austria. As Field Marshall Alexander stated in his proclamation: "The Government of the United Kingdom, the United States of America and the Union of Soviet Socialist Republics have in the declaration on Austria issued at Moscow November 1, 1943 affirmed their agreement that Austria shall be liberated from German domination, and they wish to see her re-established in freedom and independence."

This declaration is the basis of British policy towards Austria as it is that of the United States and the Soviet Union. We want to see, and we watch eagerly for every sign of a new Austria. For while the Moscow Declaration has laid down the broad principle of the intention of the United Nations, Great Britain and her Allies will be influenced not by fine words and professions of anti0German and anti-militarist sentiment, but only by Austria's own genuine contribution to her liberation. Some may say that now that the Nazi regime has vanished Austrian liberation has been achieved. But this would be taking a purely negative attitude towards the problem. We believe on the contrary that liberation is something positive, not only in the breaking of the Nazi chains but the active contribution to the reconstruction of a free Austria.

This active contribution by all Austrians of good will is vital. For the Allies can only pave the way for a free and independent Austria by destroying German militarism, the German war machine and by overthrowing Nazi rule and Nazi institutions. The actual building of a new, free and democratic Austria must be essentially the task of the Austrians themselves. At present this task can best be fulfilled, in the words of Field Marshal Alexander's proclamation, "by full Austrian cooperation with Allies forces and agencies".

Great Britain will judge the contribution which Austrians are making to their own liberation by the measure and the content of such cooperation. (TNA FO 371, 26 May 1945)

While Gaiswinkler and Grafl's role in the EBENSBURG mission has been well documented; nothing has emerged on the activities of Standhartinger and Lzicar. In a memo in early July 1945 from X.A.2 to X.AUS on the future deployment of Austrian personnel, it stated that the EBENSBURG team had not been debriefed but that Schmidt was thought to have been captured. This may well have been Karl Schmidt mentioned earlier who had been sent on a different mission. It went on to state that:

Events have recently been moving so fast that Operation Orders have almost had to be changed from hour to hour. The attached Operation Order has therefore been given to the Group concerned, and they have been given the following additional verbal instructions:

In view of the fact that their mission cannot last more than a few days the scale of operational funds has been revised. All parties will now take the total sum of RM 10,000 and $100.

All groups have been warned that they will be approached by large parties of Austrians wishing to surrender to them. They have been told that they are on no account to accept any offer of surrender without reference to this Headquarters.

Reports about the state of roads and railways in the area noting particularly where any bridges have been blown.

Collect information about troops movements paying particular attention to exact identifications.

Collect information about names and movements of any

prominent Nazis in the area and ascertain whether they have gone into hiding in the vicinity.

If they should hear that certain desperate groups of Nazis intend to make a last stand in the area, they should collect full details about those groups paying attention to their strength, location, arms etc.

They should impress upon the Austrians with whom they come into contact that every effort should be made to protect power stations, bridges, telephone lines etc.

They will report as soon as possible to the Intelligence Officer of the nearest unit with the a/m [above mentioned] information quoting the code word given in their Operation Order. (TNA HS6/22, 5 July 1945)

On 20 July, SOE was ordered to cease its paramilitary operations in Austria Villiers, mentioned earlier, was given the job of 'liquidating' SOE's agents. This was the expression used for terminating their employment and returning them to civilian life. He reported that Gaiswinkler was,

'Dropped 8 Apr 45 wrong place but made own way to BADAUSSEE and held place for four days before arrival of own troops, that the 400 resisters his party had organised. The party thus immobilised approx. one regiment of SS troops.

This man played an important part in immediately serving the organisation of civilians with occupying troops. He recovered large sums of German gold and currency for the Allies which had been concreted by the Germans in the area. He was appointed Bezirks Hauptmann [district captain and chief administrative officer of Badaussee] by the MG [Military Government] authorities and has held this post with distinction...

In view success achieved rousing and organising Austrian resisters and qualities shown in leading his party and organising Austrian civil life after the surrender, recommend on discharge: £250 and 1 suit of clothes. (TNA HS9/553/3, 12 August 1945)

Giving British troops a new suit when they were demobilised was standard military practice. In recognition of Gaiswinkler's work, SOE recommended him for the King's Medal for Brave

Conduct, but a note in his file said it was 'held pending lifting of ban on ex-enemy national.' (Ibid, 15 September 1945) The British media were unlikely to report favourably on a former member of Luftwaffe being awarded a decoration.

Grafl, Standhartinger and Lzicar had the same introductory paragraph in their reports with the additional comment that their group 'did excellent work under direction of their leader on behalf of MG during the months immediately following the general surrender of the enemy.' (HS9/606/4; HS9/1404/3; HS9/953/10)

In recognition of their efforts, it was recommended that they be given £100 each and a suit of clothes but a note in Grafl's file stated that on 25 September His Britannic Majesty's Government gave him a £50 bonus and £131 2s.5d. (5,245 Reichmarks). Grafl told Harclerode and Pittaway that he only received £45. Whether Standhartinger and Lzicar received their £100 bonus was unrecorded as a note in the SOE Summary of Austrian Claims for Assessment, dated 12 August 1945, stated that they were deferred pending deliberation in London. (Harclerode and Pittaway, op.cit. p.120) They would, however, have been able to access their pay that had been deposited in their British bank accounts.

As with Gaiswinkler, the British authorities must have been concerned about publicly rewarding former members of the German military soldiers and revealing the identities of their double agents. Grafl told Harclerode and Pittaway that none of the team received a pension or a medal from the British or the Austrians. Although the British offered him an army job after the war, he turned it down. 'Austria is free, I told them. I am happy. All four of us remained in Austria. I saw Gaiswinkler from time to time, but we hardly had anything to say to one another. I met up with the other two now and then; they had gone to live in Vienna. They're both dead as well now. I tried to get in touch with some of the others I had worked with through the British military during the war. There was no reaction.' (Ibid.) Some people in his home village treated him as an outcast because he had helped the British. 'Many people would not talk to me after the war because I was "an Englishman" to them. I couldn't make friends in Aussee because of what I had done. Whenever I walked into a bar, they would stop talking and say, "Here comes the Englander". ... It seemed to me that we all stopped mattering when that job in the mine was done.' (Ibid. pp.120-121)

Operation EBENSBURG was a mission of international importance, but although the men's heroism and bravery and the staggering value of the artworks they helped preserve have been acknowledged, Harclerode and Pittaway commented that their reward was 'pitiful to the point of being insulting.' (Ibid.) However, according to Pirker, in June 1971, Grafl received the 'Italy Star' and 'War Medal 1939 – 1945' from Wilkinson, who had been appointed British Ambassador in Vienna. (Pirker, op.cit.)

Kirstein, writing in the Town and Country magazine in autumn 1945, stated that 'so many witnesses told so many stories that the more information we accumulated, the less truth it seemed to contain'. (Charney, op.cit. p.276) Although the miners and resistance fighters had their stories to tell, it was often local officials whose accounts were documented, many of whom had collaborated with the Nazis. Charney commented that 'At the war's end, collaborating with the Allies, and sometimes inventing stories of resistance to one's Nazi colleagues, was a good strategy to avoid imprisonment. Therefore, the statements made by Nazi staff are suspect. (Charney, op.cit. p.263-4)

In November 1945, Gaiswinkler was elected a member of the Austrian Socialist Party in the first election of the National Council. Pirker 's article 'Subversion of German rule' reported that once in government, Gaiswinkler criticised the Second Republic for failing to recognise "the heroic achievements of the Austrian freedom fighters in the Ausserland. Unfortunately, the guilty gratitude to these people has not been fulfilled by fulfilling their justified demands." With the American's anti-Soviet stance, they withdrew support for left-wing elements in the new Austrian government. In 1946, private individuals, including former Nazis backed by the Americans, initiated criminal proceedings against him for abuse of official authority. The exact details of the accusation have not come to light but Grafl was reported to have claimed that Gaiswinkler benefitted financially from his involvement with the Allies. However, meticulous investigations failed to prove it and the case was dropped. Whether those Austrians who benefitted financially from confiscating Jewish property, their possessions and bank accounts, and sending them to extermination camps were criticised at that time is unknown. While SOE allocated considerable funds for the EBENSBURG mission; it is more than likely any remaining money would have been collected at the end of the war. What exactly he spent the money on is unknown, but there were suggestions that he had acquired property. Whether this was buildings or possessions confiscated from the Nazis who had fled the area or who were arrested is unknown.

The following year, his political opponents encouraged former Nazi party members to oppose his left-wing policies and in 1947, when, with the assistance of a ghostwriter, he published his wartime memoirs, *Sprung in die Freiheit, (Jump into Freedom)*, he was criticised for exaggerating his role in the liberation and saving the artworks. Grafl disputed some of his claims, particularly what happened to the wireless set, his role in the removal of the bombs, the rescue of the artworks and to have been in charge of over 300 men. However, Wilkinson mentioned his group numbering 360 and Mackenzie stated he had raised an active force of 350 men and armed them with German weapons. These criticisms led to him being deselected for the 1949 election, so he joined the Left Socialists and stood as a communist. He later returned to his previous work in health insurance as Regional Manager and died in Bad Aussee in May 1979. (https://de.wikipedia.org/wiki/Albrecht_Gaiswinkler)

While SOE, American and Austrian post-war reports gave credit to Gaiswinker, some Austrian historians follow Plieseis' claim that when the team landed, they hid and waited for the American forces to arrive. They reject Gaiswinkler's claim that he was the organiser and major of a 300-strong resistance group and dispute that he had been instrumental in removing and hiding the six bombs from the mine, saying it was the salt miners themselves. They also argue that he had nothing to do with the rescue of the works of art and abused his position to benefit financially. (Ibid; Pirker, op.cit.) However, he and his team are documented as organising the protection of the mine, using clever propaganda and disinformation to confuse the German forces in the Bad Salzkammergut area, initiating decisive military action against them, capturing German troops and their leaders as well as assisting the Americans in apprehending leading Nazi officials.

Michel claimed that it was him who informed Pearson of the mines' contents and ordered the removal of the bombs.

Historian Birgit Schwarz described Michel as 'a heavily burdened regime opportunist', who, immediately after the German surrender, entrusted the Americans as stewards of the mine 'while styling himself the saviour of the treasure.' (https://www.profil.at/home/der-salzberg-altaussee-hollywood-thriller-351944)

While it was Kaltenbrunner who countermanded Eibruger's order to destroy the mine and Pöchmüller, Raudaschl and Holger who arranged for the removal of the bombs, it was the miners who did the work. While saving a significant portion of Europe's cultural heritage would have been of some importance to the miners, they were probably more interested in saving the mine itself and securing a continued livelihood for themselves and their families.

According to Gaiswinkler's Wikipedia page, the 1968 film 'Where Eagles Dare', despite lacking source material, used parts of Gaiswinkler and Grafl's stories and locations in the Feuerkogl area. However, the agents were British and American, not Austrian. The webpage also claimed that the 1990 television film 'At the end of a long winter', based on Walter Wippersberg's book, was a better representation. (https://de.wikipedia.org/wiki/Albrecht_Gaiswinkler)

In 2009, Daniel Bernhardt, an independent video documentary maker from Bad Aussee, produced a video on Gaiswinkler entitled, 'Held oder Hochstapler' which examined the evidence for him being a hero or a fraud.

In 2013, Konrad Kramar, a journalist from the Austrian newspaper Kurier, published *Mission Michelangelo*, which investigated the events around Bad Aussee during the war and credited the mineworkers for stopping the mine's demolition, admitting that they may just have wanted to save the mines that provided jobs for them. The following year, the Hollywood film 'The Monuments Men' depicted the American rescue of the artworks but made no mention of the EBENSBURG team.

Petra Dorrmann and André Schäfer's 2015 TV documentary 'Hitlers Schatz im Berg' (Hitler's Treasure in the Mountains) retold the story of the looted artworks using interviews with historians, contemporary photographs and documents but none of the SOE files. It mentioned Gaiswinkler and Grafl, repeating the claim that Gaiswinkler, an anti-Nazi, enriched himself illegally after the war. Given the international interest, the programme was translated into French with the title 'Les

Oeuvres volées par Hitler ou incroyable sauvetage (the works stolen by Hitler or the incredible rescue).

The books, documentary and films led to the opening of the Salzwelten museum at Altaussee as a tourist attraction where visitors can enter the caverns where the artwork was stored and read the displays and watch videos about the mine's history. In September 2016, a two-day international workshop entitled 'Official appreciation of the salvation of the art treasures in the Altaussee' was held at the museum where the facts and the myths about the mine were discussed.

While people tend to remember those whose stories have been written down or have had a TV documentary or a film made about them; there are often many unnamed individuals who deserve credit. Hopefully, this book has helped acknowledge their roles. Whether Operation EBENSBURG would have failed if the German wireless set not been acquired is unknown. None of the messages sent between Grafl and Bari have come to light. Whether the Americans would have been able to rescue the art works and capture leading Nazi officers without the assistance of the EBENSBURG team is unknown. It is true though that if the team had been injured or killed when they parachuted back into Austria, captured as they descended the Zielgebiet am Zinken plateau, when they were on the train to Bad Aussee, when they were encamped in the woods or killed during confrontations with the Nazis, it is very likely Eigruber would have carried out Hitler's Nero Decree and Europe would have lost a significant portion of its cultural heritage.

Bernard O'Connor

Bibliography

Books and articles
Charney, Noah, *Stealing the Mystic Lamb: The True Story of the World's Most Coveted Masterpiece,* Public Affairs, New York, 2012
De Jaeger, Charles, *The Linz File: Hitler's Plunder of Europe's Art,* London: Webb & Bower, 1981
Gaiswinkler, Albrecht, *Sprung in die Freiheit,* Ried-Verlag, Vienna, 1947
Harclerode, Peter & Pittaway, Brendan, *The Lost Masters: The Looting of Europe's Treasurehouses,* Orion, 2000
Kramar, Konrad, *Mission Michelangelo,* Residenz Verlag, 2013
Nicholas, Lynn, *The Rape of Europa: The Fate of Europe's Treasures in the Third Reich and the Second World War,* Vintage, 1995
Mackenzie, William, *Official History of the SOE 1940-1945,* St Ermin's Press, 2001
Matteson, Robert, 'The Last Days of Ernst Kaltenbrunner,' *Studies in Intelligence,* CIA Publication, 1960, pp. A17-18
Morrison, Jim, *'The True Story of the Monuments Men,* Smithsonian.com
Pirker, Peter, *Subversion deutscher Herrschaft Der britische Kriegsgeheimdienst SOE und Österreich,* Vienna University Press, 2012)
Steinacher, Gerald, 'The Special Operations Executive (SOE) in Austria, 1940-1945', *International Journal of Intelligence & Counterintelligence,* 15, 2002
Vaughn, Cy, *Depot Dora: Stolen Masterpieces and Hidden Treasures,* Wheatmark, 2016

Youtube videos
Gaiswinkler: ein Held oder Hochstapler (a hero or swindler')
(https://www.youtube.com/watch?v=oAtY2uhEdIE)
Hitlers Schatz im Berg (https://www.youtube.com/watch?v=pk4PqZ7RDsg)
The works stolen by Hitler or the incredible rescue (http://www.dailymotion.com/video/x5kkhik)

Documents in the National Archives, Kew
FO 371 Austria

Operation EBENSBURG

FO 837/1154/3 Enemy Property outside enemy territory
FO 1020/2766/3 Allied Commission for Austria
FO 1020/1252 General Staff Intelligence (GSI(a))
Gaiswinkler's Aussee Party, Sheet 20, paras, 78-80
HS6/20 MARYLAND mission Part 3, 1945
HS6/21 MARYLAND mission Part 4, 17 April 1945 - 21 May 1945
HS6/22 MARYLAND mission Part 5 1945
HS7/146 German directorate history Part I (continued): Austria, Sudetenland)
HS8/883 Operations into Germany - Bonzos
HS9/553/3 Gaiswinkler
HS9/606/4 Grafl
HS9/953/10 Lzicar
HS9/1390/8 Sommer
HS9/1404/3 Standhartinger
WO 204/10249 Clowder Mission on future of special operations in Austria

Documents in the Imperial War Museum, Hendon
03 56/11/2/2 History of Clowder Mission. Wilkinson Papers

Websites
http://blogs.artinfo.com/outtakes/2015/03/24/fifa-art-stashed-in-castles-and-salt-mines/
https://www.profil.at/home/der-salzberg-altaussee-hollywood-thriller-351944
http://conspiracy-cafe.blogspot.co.uk/2016/12/nazi-trivia-villa-kerry-altaussee.html
https://furtherglory.wordpress.com/tag/altaussee-salt-mine/
http://www.thetimes.co.uk/article/0,,47575,00.html
https://www.profil.at/home/der-salzberg-altaussee-hollywood-thriller-351944
http://www.company7.com/bosendorfer/mauthausen/august_eigruber.html http://
azdak.livejournal.com/170003.html
https://upload.wikimedia.org/wikipedia/commons/thumb/1/14/Villa_Castiglioni_Grundlsee.jpg/1024px-Villa_Castiglioni_Grundlsee.jpg
http://www.ooegeschichte.at/epochen/oberoesterreich-in-der-zeit-des-nationalsozialismus/widerstand/widerstandsgruppen/widerstand-im-ausseergebiet.html http://

www.historiassegundaguerramundial.com/lugares/las-minas-de-sal-de-altaussee/?lang=en#prettyPhoto[979982]/0/
https://www.cia.gov/library/center-for-the-study-of-intelligence/kent-csi/vol4no2/html/v04i2a07p_0001.htm
https://www.cia.gov/library/readingroom/docs/CIA-RDP78-03921A000300300001-1.pdf
https://forum.paradoxplaza.com/forum/index.php?threads/visualizing-the-second-world-war.932086/page-9
http://www.forgottenairfields.com/uploads/airfields/italy/apulia/brindisi/brindisi_idroscalo/brindisi-idroscalo-chart-1943.jpg) https://static2.bergfex.com/images/downsized/79/f8e096f8ad7ea679_4d7b7a94a89a6208.jpg
http://www.gifex.com/fullsize-en/2011-07-04-14031/Physical-map-of-Styria.html http://oesterreichterrorismus.blogspot.com/2014/08/kriegsverbrecherjagd-im-ausseerland.html) http://www.iwm.org.uk/collections/item/object/1030014687 https://en.wikipedia.org/wiki/List_of_Special_Operations_Executive_operations#Austria; TNA HS6/18-22
http://www.ibiblio.org/pha/policy/1943/431000a.html
https://de.wikipedia.org/wiki/Josef_Hans_Grafl https://en.wikipedia.org/wiki/Albrecht_Gaiswinkler
https://de.wikipedia.org/wiki/Albrecht_Gaiswinkler
https://de.wikipedia.org/wiki/Sepp_Plieseis http://www.specialforcesroh.com/gallery.php?do=view_image&id=21608&gal=gallery
http://leicestershirelalala.com/ralph-hollingworth-our-top-brass-in-soe/ http://www.lootedart.com/P43P5J761921)
http://www.specialforcesroh.com/gallery.php http://www.army.cz/images/id_7001_8000/7419/assassination-en.pdf
http://digitalcommons.unl.edu/historyfacpub/140)
http://www.doew.at
https://www.monumentsmenfoundation.org/the-heroes/the-monuments-men/croft-murray-maj.-edward

Bernard O'Connor's publications on SOE and the Intelligence Services during the Second World War:

RAF Tempsford: Churchill's MOST SECRET Airfield, Amberley Publishing, (2010)
The Women of RAF Tempsford: Heroines of Wartime Resistance, Amberley Publishing, (2011)
Churchill and Stalin's Secret Agents: Operation Pickaxe at RAF Tempsford, Fonthill Media, (2011)
The Tempsford Academy: Churchill and Roosevelt's Secret Airfield, Fonthill Media, (2012)
Agent Rose: The true Story of Eileen Nearne, Britain's Forgotten Wartime Heroine, Amberley Publishing, (2013)
Churchill's Angels: How Britain's Women Secret Agents Changed the Course of the Second World War, Amberley Publishing, (2014)
The Courier: Reminiscences of a Female Secret Agent in Wartime France, (Historical faction) www.lulu.com (2010)
Designer: The True Story of Jacqueline Nearne, www.lulu.com, (2012)
Return to Belgium, www.lulu.com (2012)
Return to Holland, www.lulu.com, (2012)
Bedford Spy School, www.lulu.com (2012)
Old Bedfordians' Secret Operations during World War Two, www.lulu.com (2012)
Henri Dericourt: Triple Agent (edited), www.lulu.com (2012)
Churchill's School for Saboteurs: Brickendonbury, STS 17, Amberley Publishing, (2013)
Churchill's Most Secret Airfield, Amberley Publishing, (2013)
Sabotage in Norway, www.lulu.com (2013)
Sabotage in Denmark, www.lulu.com *(2013)*
Sabotage in Belgium, www.lulu.com (2013)
Sabotage in Holland, www.lulu.com (2013)
Sabotage in France, www.lulu.com (2013)
Blackmail Sabotage, www.lulu.com (2014)
Sabotage in Greece, www.lulu.com (2014)
Elzbieta Zawacka: Polish soldier and courrer during the Second World War, www.lulu.com (2014)
Agent Fifi and the Honeytrap Spies, Amberley Publishing, (2015)
Agents Françaises, www.lulu.com (2016)
The Spies who returned to the Cold: Iceland's wartime spies, www.lulu.com (2016)
Operation LENA and Hitler's Plans to blow up Britain , Amberley Publishing (2017)

Bernard O'Connor

SOE Heroines: The Special Operation Executive's French Section and Free French women agents, Amberley Publishing, (2018)
Bletchley Park and the Pigeon Spies, www.lulu.com (2018)
Bletchley Park and the Belgian Pigeon Service, www.lulu.com (2018)
The BBC and the Pigeon Spies, www.lulu.com, (2018)

Coming soon:
Sabotage on the Iberian Peninsula: the Nazi's attempts to destroy British interests in Portugal, Spain and Gibraltar
Blowing up Iberia: The British Plans for the Invasion of Iberia during the Second World War

Purchase books online:
www.lulu.com/spotlight/coprolite

Visit Bernard O'Connor's website:
www.bernardoconnor.org.uk

Email: fquirk202@aol.com

Operation EBENSBURG